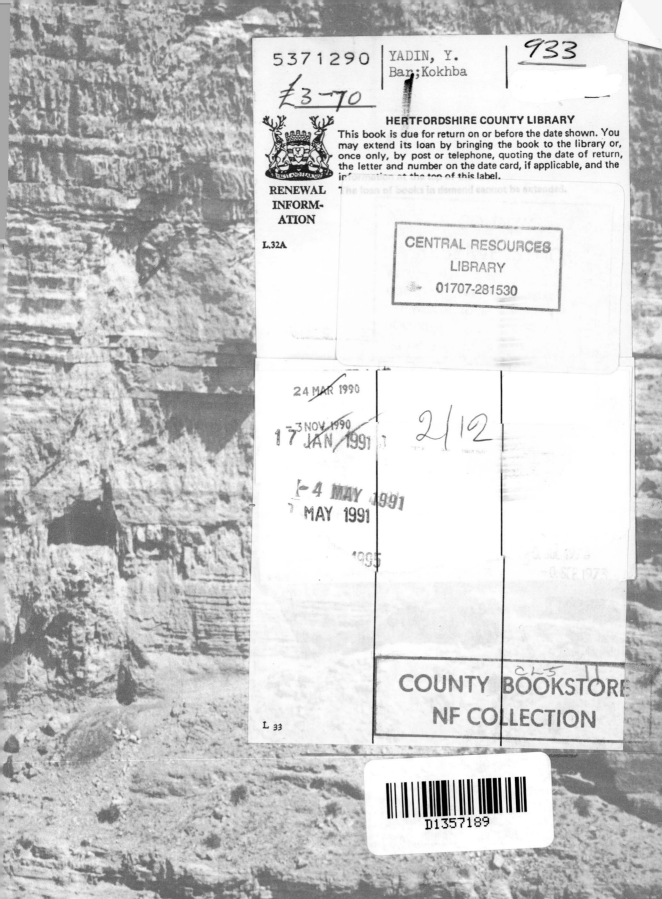

Bar-Kokhba

Bar-Kokhba

The rediscovery of the legendary hero of the last
Jewish Revolt against Imperial Rome

Yigael Yadin

The Hebrew University of Jerusalem

Weidenfeld and Nicolson

Weidenfeld and Nicolson
5 Winsley Street London W1

Weidenfeld and Nicolson Jerusalem
19 Herzog Street Jerusalem

ISBN 0 297 00345 3

Photoset by BAS Printers Limited,
Wallop, Hampshire, England
Printed at Japhet Press, Tel Aviv,
and bound at
Wiener Bindery, Jerusalem

Title page:
The bundle of the Bar-Kokhba
letters as found in the cave

Frontispiece: Jugs, a key and a mirror
found in the Cave of Letters in the
Nahal Hever canyon
(*photograph : David Harris*)

To my daughters Orly and Littal

Contents

List of maps

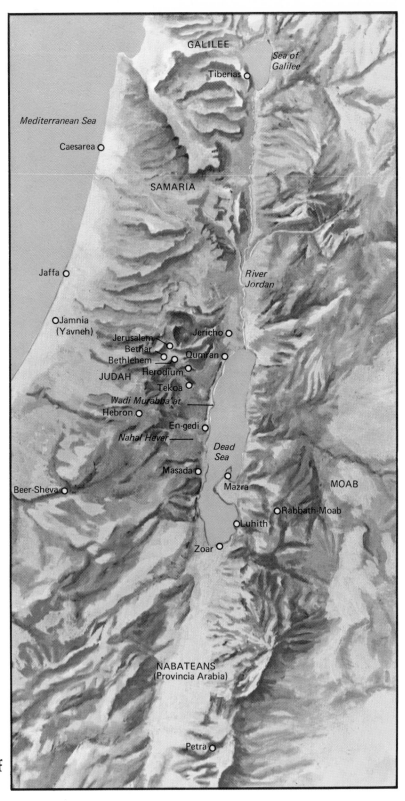

Palestine at the time of Bar-Kokhba

Bethar

Jerusalem

Herodium

Qumran

Masada

Wadi Murabba´at

Nahal Hever

Zoar

Petra

River Jordan

Dead Sea

Historical sites connected with the First and Second Revolts

Preface

Sometimes the most important discoveries are made accidentally, in which case the finds themselves are the only things that matter. But sometimes an archaeologist embarks on a special expedition with a specific object in mind, and when this is attained, the 'why' and 'how' are nearly as important, and certainly as exciting, as the discovery itself. Such was the case of the Bar-Kokhba expedition – the subject of this book.

In the following pages I have striven, therefore, to let the reader share with the archaeologists, their thoughts, planning, frustrations and joys before, and during, the two short seasons of digging in the remote caves of the Judaean Desert. This is particularly justified I believe, in this case, since our difficulties in reaching the caves and working in them – albeit with the help of modern technology – were but a fraction of the difficulties suffered by the ancient inmates of those caves, who took refuge there with their families, when their revolt against the Romans failed in AD 135.

The reader will surely not fail to detect the excitement that pervaded us throughout, which occasionally exceeded that encountered in routine archaeological excavations. I deliberately refrained from curbing the expression of these feelings, which were natural to us not only as archaeologists, but as human beings and as Jews. After all, we were in search of – and found – the actual evidence of a lost semi-legendary hero of Israel.

This book follows the pattern of my book *Masada*, in which the text and illustrations complement each other, to form one inseparable entity. In fact the pictures are intended to play the same role as slides in an illustrated lecture. I am deeply indebted therefore, to Mr John Curtis and Miss Martha Bates of Weidenfeld and Nicolson, who very patiently bore with my whims and made useful suggestions to achieve that end. My special thanks go to Mr Trevor Vincent, who artistically and intelligently wove the pictures into the text. Most of the black-and-white pictures of the first season, were taken by R. Erde, E. Hirshbain and M. Kneller, while those of the second season are the work of Werner Braun and David Harris; the latter also took many of the photographs of the objects. I am also grateful to Mr Y. Yannai, Director of the Israel National Parks Authority and Dr A. Biran, Director of the Department of Antiquities, for the photographs of Herodium and Bethar respectively, and Père R. de Vaux for permission to reproduce the documents from Murabba'at. The general colour pictures as well as the aerial photographs are my own.

Many people have contributed in their various specialised fields to the research which made this book possible. They are mentioned in my official scientific report, *Finds from the Bar-Kokhba Period in the Cave of Letters*, published through the generous help of Mr Charles Clore of London. Readers more deeply interested in any aspect dealt with here, may refer to the above publication or to the bibliography and sources at the end of this book.

I am very grateful to Carmella, my wife, who not only shared the prosaic worries of pre- and post-expedition burdens, but rendered my poor English style readable to the extent that enabled my good friend Ronald Harker to give it a final touch. While doing so, Mr Harker, as a lay reader, forced me to elucidate a number of points. I am also indebted to Mr David Goodblatt for help in preparing the Appendix.

If I have succeeded in conveying to the reader even a fraction of the excitement and joy I derived from the expedition and from recounting it in this book – I shall have achieved my purpose and feel amply rewarded.

YIGAEL YADIN

The beginning of the wooden letter
which reads 'Shimeon Bar Kosiba,
President over Israel'

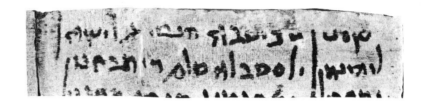

One day in the spring of 1960 I sat in my study in Jerusalem gazing at a bundle of ancient papyri, wondering what they might disclose and yet being unable to unroll them without expert aid lest they crumble to dust. They had been found in a remote cave in one of the canyons leading down towards the Dead Sea in the wilderness of Judaea. A few weeks later the papyri had been unrolled, and for a little while thereafter I was possessed of a momentous secret.

All excavations in the Holy Land are exciting, for nowhere else on earth are archaeologists probing a richer historical dust. And there has grown up a custom for the President of Israel to invite archaeologists to his home from time to time to report on their discoveries. To one of these meetings in 1960 were invited all the leaders of an expedition of four teams searching caves in the Judaean Desert. It was to be attended by the Prime Minister, then Mr David Ben-Gurion, Cabinet ministers, Members of the Knesset, and distinguished writers and other guests. I had led one of the four teams and I set out for the President's home with my secret in my brief case.

A screen had been erected at Mr Ben Zvi's house, and when my turn came to report, I projected on to the screen through a film slide the coloured photograph of part of a document and read out aloud the first line of writing upon it: 'Shimeon Bar Kosiba, President over Israel'. And turning to our Head of State, I said, 'Your Excellency, I am honoured to be able to tell you that we have discovered fifteen despatches written or dictated by the last President of ancient Israel 1800 years ago.'

For a moment the audience seemed to be struck dumb. Then the silence was shattered with spontaneous cries of astonishment and joy. That evening the national radio interrupted its scheduled programme to broadcast news of the discovery. Next day the newspapers came out with banner headlines over the announcement.

Why was this such an electrifying occasion in Jerusalem? Why was a whole nation elated over the discovery of a name on a fragment of papyrus?

The answer lies in the magic of the name, a name treasured in folklore but almost lost to authenticated history, and the realisation at this meeting that after nearly two thousand years the desert had given up factual links with the man who led the last attempt of his people to overthrow their Roman masters. This book is an account of the expedition and the dramatic discoveries that it brought about . . .

1 Behind the legend

'Judaea Capta'

The Great War of the Jews against the Romans which began in AD 66 and ended in 70 – the so-called First Revolt – was quelled with terrible consequences for Judaea. Jerusalem was conquered by Titus and destroyed, and the Temple – the centre of all Jewish national and religious activities – was demolished. A few years later the last resistance of the Jews was overcome at the rock fortress of Masada in the Judaean desert; arches of triumph were erected in Rome to commemorate the victory against Judaea and coins with inscriptions 'Judaea Capta' were in currency throughout the Roman Empire. But the Jews were not crushed. At Yavneh (Jamnia) a new centre of religious studies was being founded under the leadership of the great Rabbi Yohanan ben Zakkai and Judaism learned to survive, bereft of the Temple, the centre of its cult. New interpretations of the Law were formulated and new rules promulgated. It was here in fact that the foundations of Judaism, as we know it today, were laid. But living without the Temple and Jerusalem was regarded by all as a temporary phase. Every Jew believed in his heart that the day of his return to Jerusalem was not far off, that the Temple would be rebuilt and the Messiah would appear to redeem his people.

Unrest in the Diaspora

Outside the Holy Land meanwhile, a new Diaspora was growing. The existing Jewish communities in exile were reinforced by new refugees – among them militants who survived the First Revolt – and fresh centres of Jewish learning sprouted throughout the Roman Empire. On the surface everything seemed calm, but beneath it the old spirit of Judaism smouldered, and occasionally flamed into hostilities between the Jews and their neighbours inside and outside Palestine. Barely forty years had elapsed since the fall of Masada, and again the whole Roman Empire seemed ablaze with Jews fighting for their spiritual and religious independence in various places. This spasmodic revolt started in AD 115 in Cyrenaica, where the Jews under the leadership of a 'king' named Loukuas-Andreas fought against the local population so fiercely that eventually the Romans were compelled to intervene. At the same time, or shortly thereafter, the Jews of Egypt rose too; Cyprus followed as a battle scene, and so did Mesopotamia with a general revolt in 116. These revolts of 115–17 took place mainly in the Diaspora, but possibly some unrest filtered through also to Palestine itself. The Roman commander who finally crushed the revolt in Mesopotamia was L. Quietus, a Romanised Moor who was later appointed governor of Palestine. In some of the Jewish sources there is a reference to the 'Polemos of Quietus', the 'War of

opposite People in a besieged city throwing stones at attacking Romans; a drawing from a relief on the triumphal column of Trajan (Roman Emperor from AD 98 to 117) in Rome

17

Quietus'. The fact that Quietus was eventually sent to Palestine indicates that it, too, must have been restive. However, at that time, so it seems, the chief scenes of disturbance and insurrection were in the Diaspora.

Many explanations have been suggested for these revolts, and it is quite possible that in each place local fighting had different local causes; but it seems that the late Professor Tcherikover – an authority on the Diaspora in the Second Temple period – was right in ascribing the 'revolt of the Diaspora' not to any tangible, rational cause, but to roots in the Messianic yearnings of the Jews.

The Second Revolt

Fifteen years later, sixty-two years after the destruction of Jerusalem, a fresh revolt erupted against the Romans, this time in the Holy Land itself. The war of Bar-Kokhba, or the so-called Second Revolt, was a cruel war, perhaps more cruel than the First Revolt of 66–70. It lasted over three years with initial success for the Jews who, led by Bar-Kokhba, conquered Jerusalem and re-established the Jewish state, thus endangering the Roman Empire under Hadrian who was forced to despatch the best of his legions to Palestine to fight the rebels. Alas, this Second Revolt lacked a Josephus Flavius – the brilliant Jewish historian who described so vividly the events of the First Revolt – and thus, despite its tremendous importance, very little was known of it. All we had were a few references by some of the classical historians describing the reign of Hadrian; scattered allusions in some of the writings of the early Church Fathers recording the history of the Church and Jerusalem; and even less precise and more legendary descriptions in the Jewish sources, the Talmud and the Midrash.

'Son of a star' or 'son of a liar'

The information was so scanty that even the very name of the leader of the revolt, Bar-Kokhba, could not be ascertained. The name Bar-Kokhba – which in Hebrew or Aramaic literally means 'son of a star' obviously referring to his Messianic nature – was preserved only in the sources of the early Church Fathers. In Jewish sources on the other hand, he is referred to as Bar (or Ben) Koziba, which, though not much different in pronunciation, is quite different in meaning, i.e. 'son of a liar' or 'deceiver'. Scores of scholars have argued and debated this point for many years. One school of thought believed that his real name had indeed been Bar-Kokhba (perhaps after his birth-place) but was later, when his mission failed, altered – pun-fashion – to mean 'the deceiver'. Others argued just the reverse: that his real name had been Bar-Koziba – again after his birth-place or perhaps his father's name – later to be changed by his followers and ardent believers in his Messianic mission into Bar-Kokhba: 'son of a star'. The famous saying of the great Rabbi Aqiba, as preserved in the Talmud and the Midrash, has been quoted in support of this latter view: 'Rabbi Simon ben Yohai said: "Rabbi Aqiba my teacher, expounded the passage 'There shall go forth a star (KWKB) out of

A bust of Hadrian, Roman Emperor from AD 117 to 138

Jacob [Numbers 24:17]' as follows: There goes KWZBA out of Jacob." ' Moreover, Rabbi Aqiba is actually quoted as saying about Bar-Kokhba: 'This is the King Messiah.' We were equally uncertain about the rebellion he led, where it started, what were its actual causes, and where its main battles were fought. Let us therefore recount in brief the little which was known from the few sources available. (Texts of these sources are given in the Appendix.)

Non-Jewish sources

The most important and extensive of the classical sources for the Second Revolt are the writings of Dio Cassius, the third-century historian, in his *Roman History*, although his passage dealing with our subject actually comes to us only in an abbreviated form through the hands of Xiphilinus, an eleventh-century monk. Dio tells us that Hadrian founded in Jerusalem a city to replace the one razed to the ground, and named it Aelia Capitolina (after himself, whose complete name was Publius Aelius Hadrianus) and on the site of the Jewish Temple he erected a new temple dedicated to the Roman god Jupiter. This, according to Dio, caused a war of 'no slight importance nor of brief duration', since the Jews could not tolerate foreign races settling in their city and foreign religious rights being planted there. However, as long as Hadrian was close by in Egypt and in Syria, they remained quiet, but even at that

time – according to Dio – 'they purposely made of poor quality
such weapons as they were called upon to furnish, in order that the
Romans might reject them and they themselves might thus have
the use of them'. Actual war began only when Hadrian departed.
The Jews did not wish to risk open battle with the Romans, and
so they seized strategic places, fortified them by walls and underground tunnels to serve as potential refuge places and means of
communication when open roads were to be avoided. At the

beginning, says Dio, the Romans did not pay much attention to these activities; but when the whole of Judaea rebelled and even Jews throughout the world joined hands with the rebels (as did many non-Jews who helped because of their lust for booty) thus causing the Romans a lot of trouble – in fact when the whole empire seemed to be collapsing – only then did Hadrian decide to tackle the problem in military fashion. He therefore sent against the rebels his best commanders, foremost amongst them Julius Severus, governor of Britain, who – once he saw the multitudes of the Jews and their desperate way of fighting – refrained from face to face war. Instead he rounded up groups of them, or besieged them in cities to prevent their getting food; and thus he managed, slowly but surely, to diminish their numbers until only a few survived. Fifty fortresses – according to Dio – and 985 of the most important settlements were destroyed by the Romans; 580,000 people were slaughtered in the many skirmishes and those who died of hunger and sickness and fire were innumerable. 'Thus nearly the whole of Judaea was made desolate, a result of which the people had been forewarned before the war. For the tomb of Solomon, which the Jews regard as an object of veneration, fell to pieces of itself and collapsed. . . .'

But perhaps the most important piece of information in Dio's description is recorded at its end and deserves verbatim quotation: 'Many Romans, moreover, perished in this war. Therefore Hadrian in writing to the Senate did not employ the opening phrase commonly affected by the Emperors: "If you and your children are in health, it is well; I and the legions are in health." ' Hadrian must have suffered heavy casualties indeed if he was forced to omit the customary formula: *mihi et legionibus bene*. But Dio does not mention the leader of the Jews nor the fact that he had been successful; nor does he mention the duration of the war. In fact, even the cause of the revolt as described by Dio is contradicted by other historians. Dio attributes it directly to Hadrian's decision to build Aelia Capitolina on the ruins of Jerusalem and to erect a temple to Jupiter. Spartianus – Hadrian's biographer who lived at the end of the third century – on the other hand, ascribes the revolt in his *De Vita Hadriani*, to Hadrian's order not to 'mutilate their genitals', i.e. his prohibition of circumcision. This prohibition may possibly not have been intended specifically against the Jews but it obviously affected them more than any other people. The history of this prohibition is interesting to follow: it started before Hadrian with the Emperor Domitian, who banned castration, a rule repeated also by the Emperor Nerva. Hadrian later interpreted this to include circumcision, and thus in his reign both castration and circumcision were considered capital offences. A third possible cause for the revolt, as seen by some historians, is a strange reference in one of the Midrashim to the fact that at one time Hadrian had

opposite above (left to right) A coin of Bar-Kokhba with the inscription 'Shimeon President of Israel'; a 'Judaea Capta' coin; a coin with the inscription 'Colonia Aelia Capitolina condita' (i.e. the founding of the colony Aelia Capitolina)
opposite below Reverse sides of the above coins (left to right): inscription reading 'Year One of the Redemption of Israel'; bust of Emperor Vespasian; a bust of Hadrian

agreed to rebuild the Jewish Temple in Jerusalem but later changed his mind because of complaints by the Samaritans.

How little is actually agreed upon about the real causes of the revolt may be learned from the fact that quite recently one scholar (Hugo Mantel) came to the conclusion that 'not the decrees of Hadrian . . . caused the Bar-Kokhba revolt, but the reverse is true: Hadrian's decree constituted a reaction of the Romans to the Jewish Revolt'. In this, in fact, he follows Pausanius who ascribed the Second Revolt to the general disobedience and revolutionary tendencies of the Jews who were actually longing for the restoration of their independent state. In addition to the meagre information gathered from classical sources, a little more can be learned, with due caution of course, from some of the writings of the early Fathers of the Church, most important of which are those of Eusebius, Bishop of Caesaria, in the third and fourth centuries. Eusebius points out that the then governor of Judaea, Rufus, after receiving reinforcements dispatched to his aid by Hadrian, dealt with the revolt very cruelly, killing thousands of men, women and children. At that time, according to Eusebius, the commander of the Jews was a man by the name of Bar Chochebas, which, Eusebius adds, means 'the star'. This man, he continues, was no more than a bandit, but because of his name he managed to attract the simple people and persuade them that he came from heaven to redeem the suffering (i.e. that he was a Messiah). The war 'reached its height in the eighteenth year of the reign of Hadrian in Bethera [Bethar], which was a strong citadel not very far from Jerusalem. The siege lasted a long time before the rebels were driven to final destruction by famine and thirst.' Hadrian's Year 18 is normally reckoned as 134–5. Eusebius goes on to record that later the Jews, by special decree of Hadrian, were banned from the district of Jerusalem and were in fact prohibited from approaching within sight of it. From then on Jerusalem was inhabited by gentiles and named Aelia in honour of the Emperor. Eusebius, whose main concern in his books is naturally the history of the Church, adds that from then on the Christian Church of Jerusalem was headed by the first gentile bishop, Marcus. He also quotes another Christian source contemporary to the revolt, Justin Martyr, as saying that Bar-Kokhba particularly persecuted the Christians.

Some more information concerning Bar-Kokhba is contained in Eusebius's *Chronicle* as preserved in the Latin recension by Jerome. The events are recorded year by year. Under Year 16 of Hadrian, he mentions the fact that the Jews revolted and destroyed Palestine at the time of the governor Tineus Rufus. It was to him, according to Eusebius, that Hadrian that year sent reinforcements in order to subdue the revolt. In the following year, says Eusebius, Chochebas, the leader of the Jewish sect, killed Christians because they refused to join his revolt against the Romans, and under the Year 18

(Armenian version: 19) he says that the Jewish war came to its end and the Jewish revolt was completely quelled, after which the Jews were prevented from entering Jerusalem.

Quite a number of references to Bar-Kokhba and the Second Revolt are to be found in the writings of Jerome (fourth-fifth centuries), who also translated some of Eusebius's works, and like him wrote a history of the Church; he seems to have known personally several Jewish scholars of his times, and incorporated some Jewish traditions in his writings. In his commentary on the Bible he occasionally inserts references to Bar-Kokhba and the Second Revolt. In fact he sees references to events of the revolt and what happened to the Jews in the books of Isaiah, Jeremiah, Ezekiel and Joel. In his commentary to Isaiah 2:15, he says that that verse actually alludes to the great victories of the Romans over the Jews in both the First and Second Revolts and adds a very interesting piece of information at the end. He says that the people of Judaea suffered to such a degree during that war that they were compelled to seek refuge in underground crevices and deep caves together with their wives and children. This is worth remembering in the light of recent archaeological exploration in the Judaean Desert.

A glance at the Jewish sources related to Bar-Kokhba, assembled in the Appendix, shows immediately how they differ from the sources already mentioned. Except for the very scanty and meagre bits of information of a purely historical nature, most of them are legendary in character, albeit with some historical core. In *Seder Olam* (a chronological essay) we read: 'From the Polemos of Quietus until the war of Ben Koziba – sixteen years; and the war of Ben Koziba – three years and a half.' The Polemos of Quietus, as already mentioned, refers to the revolts in the Diaspora in 115–17. According to this treatise, therefore, the war of Bar-Kokhba began about 132 and continued into 135. This also tallies with what we know from other sources. In another reference in Talmudic literature, the duration of the war, or rather of the 'Kingdom' of Bar-Kokhba, is indicated as two and a half years. Earlier on we have quoted the great Rabbi Aqiba who expounded 'There shall go forth a star (KWKB) out of Jacob' and 'There goes KWZBA out of Jacob' and said of Bar-Kokhba: 'This is the King Messiah.' Not all shared Rabbi Aqiba's belief, as indicated by Rabbi Yohanan ben Tortha's reply to him: 'Aqiba, grass will grow in your jawbones and he [the son of David] will still not have come.' Many of the passages tell of Bar-Kokhba's extraordinary bravery, his toughness and his brutality. Probably such descriptions emanated from his opponents or from the disillusion of his final defeat and failure. There is a story of his practice to test the prowess of his soldiers by cutting off their fingers. The sages used to tell him: 'How long will you continue to make the men of Israel blemished?' When he

Jewish sources

23

Bronze coins of Bar-Kokhba.
above The inscriptions read:
(top row, left to right)
'Year One of the Redemption'
of Israel': 'Shimeon'; 'Shimeon';
(bottom row, left to right)
'Year Two of the Freedom of Israel':
'Year One of the Redemption of
Israel'; 'Eleazar the priest'
below Other sides of the above
coins. The inscriptions read:
(top row, left to right)
'Shimeon President of Israel';
'of the Freedom of Jerusalem';
'of the Freedom of Jerusalem';
(bottom row, left to right)
'Jerusalem';
'Shimeon President of Israel';
'of the freedom of Jerusalem'

Silver coins of Bar-Kokhba.
above (top row) Two silver *tetra-drachmas* both with a *lulav* and the inscription 'of the Freedom of Jerusalem' (left) and 'Year Two of the Freedom of Israel'
(bottom row) four silver *dinars* with the inscriptions (left to right): 'Shimeon'; 'of the Freedom of Jerusalem'; 'Shime[on]'; 'Shimeon'
below Other sides of the above coins. (top row, left to right) The façade of the Temple with the inscription 'Shimeon'; the façade of the Temple with the inscription 'Jerusalem'. Note the star above the building. (bottom row, left to right) 'Year Two of the Freedom of Israel'; 'Shimeon'; Eleazar the priest'; two trumpets and the inscription 'of the Freedom of Jerusalem'

retorted: 'How else shall they be tested?' they replied: 'Let anyone who cannot uproot a cedar from Lebanon be refused enrolment in your army.' These sources add that his force numbered 400,000 tested soldiers. His own personal courage is described thus: in battle he used to bounce the ballistae stones back against his enemies with his knee, thus killing several of them. Some sources ascribe to him certain traits of conceit, even blasphemy: 'When they went forth to battle, they cried: [Oh, God!] Neither help us nor disgrace us.' His brutality, according to some sources, was manifested in the way he killed the revered Rabbi Eleazar of Modi'in, who was with him at Bethar during the last siege of the revolt, but whom Bar-Kokhba suspected of betraying the secrets of Bethar to the Romans. He 'kicked him with his foot and killed him'. This cruel act, according to the same sources, caused Bar-Kokhba's death and the fall of Bethar: 'A heavenly voice issued forth and proclaimed . . . thou hast paralysed the arm of Israel and blinded their right eye. . . . Forthwith the sins caused Bethar to be captured. Bar-Kosiba was slain . . . .'

Many of the Midrashim describe in detail the calamities which befell Bethar and the cruelty of Hadrian: 'Emperor Hadrian who slew eighty thousand myriads [!!] of human beings at Bethar . . . they [the Romans] slew the inhabitants until the horses waded up to the nostrils and the blood . . . flowed into the sea. . . .' Other atrocities are mentioned, such as the brains of three hundred children which were found on one stone and the Roman practice of wrapping children in the holy books and setting them on fire. There are lengthy descriptions of the multitudes of the slain, and Hadrian's refusal to allow them a decent burial. Another group of sources tries to explain the causes of the revolt. Although there are a lot of contradictions and obvious legends, they definitely reflect some of the incidents during, or just prior to, the actual war. A typical example is the story of how Bethar was destroyed because of a carriage axle. A custom prevailed to plant a cedar tree on the occasion of a male birth and a pine tree for a new-born female. When a young man and woman became betrothed, their cedar and pine were felled and the wood used to make a bridal canopy. One day, the Emperor's daughter passed by and the axle of her carriage broke. Her attendants felled a nearby cedar for its repair. This enraged the local inhabitants and they attacked the attendants who promptly told the Emperor that the Jews had revolted against him, so he came and attacked them.

The Bar-Kokhba coins

Talmudic sources also refer quite frequently to what they call 'Kozbian coins', and indeed the coins of Bar-Kokhba, of which thousands have been found, were the only tangible evidence we had of the Second Revolt. All of Bar-Kokhba's coins – both silver and bronze – are struck upon Roman coins. Occasionally the figures and inscriptions of the Roman coins can be seen through the

Hebrew characters. The coins, chronologically speaking, can be grouped into three types bearing the following inscriptions: (1) 'Year One of the Redemption of Israel'; (2) 'Year Two of the Freedom of Israel'; (3) undated inscription 'of the Freedom of Jerusalem'. There is a debate among scholars whether the third type was struck in Year Three, or at the very beginning of the revolt. Many of the coins bear the given name of Bar-Kokhba: 'Shimeon', sometimes with the additional title 'President [or Prince: *Nasi*] of Israel'. Before the last discoveries this was the only source which preserved his first name. Some of the coins of the first year bear another name: 'Eleazar the Priest'. On many of the coins the name of Jerusalem appears quite conspicuously. Of great interest also are the emblems which are struck on the coins, all indicating the Messianic nature of the war, and the craving for the restoration of Jerusalem and its Temple: a façade of the Temple; the *lulav* (palm branch) and *ethrog* (citron); an oil-libation jug; a bunch of grapes; a palm tree; a vine leaf; the holy trumpets and other holy musical instruments. The coins are beautifully designed and well made – considering that they were struck in haste – and are a tangible testimony to the pride and joy of those who issued them. The plates show most of the known types of Bar-Kokhba's silver and bronze coins.

The allusions to Bar-Kokhba in the Jewish sources are, as we saw, ambivalent in nature: animosity towards a 'Messiah' who failed, combined with awe and admiration for a military hero. Legend has it that even Hadrian could not help admiring Bar-Kokhba's prowess and his charismatic leadership: 'Bar Koziba was slain and his head taken to Hadrian. "Who killed him?" asked Hadrian. A Samaritan said: "I killed him." "Bring his body to me," he ordered. He went and found a snake encircling its neck, so [Hadrian] exclaimed: "If his God had not slain him, who could have overcome him?" '

But when all the fragmentary tales and traces of Bar-Kokhba were assembled they amounted to no more than the lineaments of a ghost. He figured in Jewish folklore more as a myth than a man of flesh and blood, as impersonal as a Hercules or a King Arthur. It was centuries of persecution of the Jews and their yearning for national rehabilitation that turned Bar-Kokhba into a people's hero – an elusive figure they clung to because he had demonstrated, and was the last to demonstrate, that the Jews could fight to win spiritual and political independence. To commemorate his revolt it became traditional for the children of Jewish communities in eastern Europe to go into the fields at the festival of Lag Ba'omer and play 'Bar-Kokhba and the Romans' with makeshift bows and arrows, as Western children play cowboys and indians or Robin Hood. For a short while they were thus transported from the Diaspora to the land of their ancestors, dreaming. . . .

A legendary hero

2 The curtain rises

Wadi Murabba'at –
great discoveries

The discovery of the famous Dead Sea Scrolls in the caves of Qumran on the north-west shore of the Dead Sea, in the late forties, had a tremendous impact also on their first discoverers – the Bedouins of the Ta'amireh tribe. The importance of the scrolls – at least their financial importance – was not lost on them and many of them had turned from a tribe of shepherds to a tribe of amateur archaeologists, or rather antiquities' hunters. Towards the end of 1951, these Bedouins stumbled on a discovery which – had it been made earlier or had it been the only find in the Dead Sea area – might have excited the scholarly world at the time, almost as much as the discovery of the Dead Sea Scrolls did four years earlier. In October 1951, some of these Bedouins offered for sale to the Palestine Archaeological (Rockefeller) Museum in Jerusalem (at that time under Jordanian rule) a few fragments of inscribed leather, bearing some Hebrew and Greek words. When asked about their provenance, the Bedouins conducted Mr Joseph Sa'ad, the Museum's secretary, to a big cave in the Judaean Desert – in a canyon called Wadi Murabba'at – near the shores of the Dead Sea, about eighteen kilometres as the crow flies south of the first cave of Qumran, about eight kilometres west of it, and roughly three kilometres from the sea. Some time later a few members of the American School of Oriental Research in Jerusalem visited the cave, but noticing that it had already been excavated and because the fragments offered seemed insignificant, they did not pursue their quest further. During November of that year, while Mr Lankester Harding, then Director of Antiquities in Jordan, and Père R. de Vaux, Director of the École Biblique et Archéologique Française, were busy digging Khirbet Qumran near the famous caves, Khalil Iskandar Shahin – better known as Kando, the dealer from Bethlehem who was notorious for his role in the acquisition of the first Dead Sea Scrolls – offered to sell Père de Vaux various fragments, assuring him that they too had come from the Qumran caves. The material seemed different to de Vaux, and when he pressed Kando, the dealer admitted that it came from elsewhere, though not far away from those caves. On 9 December, de Vaux bought from Kando some of these documents. Among them was a papyrus beginning with the words: 'From Shimeon to Yeshua ben Galgoula, *Shalom* [greetings].' In January 1952, de Vaux and Harding bought from Kando and from the Bedouins of the Ta'amireh tribe some more documents, including another that began similarly: 'From Shimeon ben Kosiba to Yeshua ben

Galgoula and the people of the fort, *Shalom*.' It was obvious that they belonged to the Bar-Kokhba period; indeed, they revealed for the first time his true name: Shimeon ben (or bar) Kosiba. We could now understand the riddle of his name. Those who, like Rabbi Aqiba, believed in his Messianic nature called him – playing a small pun on his name by changing the S into Kh – Kokhba; while those who opposed him, particularly after his failure, played a different pun by changing the S into Z, thus distorting the meanings completely to read 'liar' or 'son of a liar'.

With wit and typical oriental bargaining Père de Vaux managed after long conversations and negotiations, to persuade some of the Ta'amireh Bedouins to show him the actual cave where these precious documents had been found. It turned out to be a cave in Wadi Murabba'at. In fact when de Vaux and Harding arrived at the caves they saw many Bedouins – thirty-four to be exact – fleeing from their illicit exploration there. They had obviously been working for weeks. In difficult conditions Harding and de Vaux now explored these remote caves from 21 January to 1 March 1952. They found four caves in all, two of them quite large and about fifty metres long, one of which – now known as Cave 2 – was the more important. A superficial examination of the caves proved at once that they were indeed the source of the abundance of documents on the market. Although the Bedouins had roamed the area for several weeks and discovered most of the documents, the excavations were still of extreme importance because, besides finding additional documents, it was quickly established that these

The caves of Wadi Murabba'at, looking north, where the first Bar-Kokhba documents were found by the Bedouins

caves had been in use not only in Roman times but thousands of years earlier. Remains were found there of the Chalcolithic Age (the transitional period between the Stone and Copper Ages, at the end of the fourth millenium BC), of the Middle Bronze Age – the period of the Hebrew Patriarchs (in the middle of the second millenium) and of the so-called Iron Age (in the eighth-seventh centuries BC) – which was the time of the Kings of Judah. It became quite clear that these remote caves, like those to be discovered and described later, served as places of refuge throughout the ages for people who were forced by circumstances to flee the rulers of the land.

Shortly afterwards other documents of the same style were offered for sale by the Bedouins to scientific institutions in Jordan's Jerusalem. These documents were referred to by scholars in Jordan as coming from 'an unknown source'. It seemed evident to everybody, however, that this source could be none other than caves across the border, inside Israel. After all, for nomadic Bedouins a border is no barrier!

At this point, let us leave these activities in Jordan and transfer our attention to what happened from then on in Israel.

Nahal Hever – great disappointment

Before the news of the discoveries of Wadi Murabba'at reached Israel, the late Professor E. L. Sukenik – the first scholar to recognise the antiquity and scientific value of the Dead Sea Scrolls – planned a survey of the caves in the Israeli part of the Judaean Desert west of the Dead Sea, with special emphasis on the region of the oasis of En-gedi. This was with the definite purpose of discovering written documents. However, Sukenik's illness and subsequent untimely death early in 1953 prevented him from carrying out his plans. When the first sensational news about the discovery of the Bar-Kokhba documents in Wadi Murabba'at – and the possibility that some other documents were actually found by Bedouins in caves within Israel – reached the Israelis, it created an exciting stir.

The first person to take the initiative in examining the caves in the vicinity of En-gedi was a certain Mr Uri Shoshani, an amateur explorer. While still in the midst of his explorations near En-gedi, Shoshani received word of Bedouin activities in the nearby caves of Nahal Hever, a few kilometres to the south. As a result of this information Y. Aharoni (now Professor Aharoni), then inspector of the Israeli Department of Antiquities, entered the field with the assistance of his department and the Israel Defence Forces, and conducted a survey in Nahal Hever. This survey lasted twenty days, from 25 November to 16 December 1953, and centred on examination of the caves. Because of the difficult terrain and the lack of roads in the area, most of the supplies and equipment were carried to the site on the backs of mules or the backs of the surveyors themselves. Scrutiny of some of these caves immediately showed that they had already been explored by the Bedouins. In many places not only were there clear traces of digging, but actual written material in Arabic such as cigarette boxes manufactured in Jordan was found. Nevertheless, enough was discovered to indicate that the caves had indeed been occupied in both the Chalcolithic period and the Roman period, i.e. during the Bar-Kokhba Revolt too, just like the caves in Wadi Murabba'at. This was particularly apparent from the many broken jars and sherds scattered all over the cave, which the Bedouins left untouched. After all, of what interest could broken pottery be? However, the members of the team made one discovery of which the significance became evident only many years later, as shall be recounted in due course. On the northern bank of Nahal Hever, in the cliffs, they discovered a huge cave, above which there were clear remains of a Roman siege camp; and similar remains were visible above another cave on the southern bank, more or less across from the first cave. Evidently the besieged people in those caves must have been of some importance to the Romans if they bothered to besiege them in this remote spot. With great difficulty did the members of the team manage to penetrate the big cave in the north, only to discover to their dismay that the Bedouins had preceded them even into this least accessible of caves. Again cigarette boxes manufactured in Jordan awaited them, as well as traces of digging, broken jars, discarded bits of clothing, mats and so forth. Considerable parts of the floor of the cave were strewn with huge boulders fallen from the ceiling, which could not be moved and it was of course dangerous to blow them up. This, and the fact that the Bedouins had already explored the cave, prompted the expedition to renounce any further investigation there and to return to Jerusalem. One conclusion was clear: caves did exist, but the Bedouins seemed always to forestall the scholars.

In 1955 (2 to 9 May) Aharoni returned to explore Nahal Hever, his main object this time being the other cave, on the southern bank of the canyon, with remains of a Roman siege camp. Perhaps – he hoped – the Bedouins might have failed to enter a cave so hard to reach. With great difficulties, using ropes and ladders, the team at last gained access to the cave, only to be disappointed yet again. Even here the Bedouins had come first! Nevertheless, some remains from the Bar-Kokhba period were found, including scores of skeletons and skulls of men, women and children, evidently the remains of fighters for Bar-Kokhba who took refuge there with their families. The sight of these skeletons confronting the first members of the team was so horrifying that the team subsequently labelled that cave the 'Cave of Horrors'. The fact that the busy Bedouins had gained access to even this almost unreachable cave caused despair among Israeli scholars, and all further survey and exploration in the Judaean Desert caves were abandoned, except for minor activity around En-gedi in 1956.

Another disappointment

3 First rays of hope

Nahal Se'elim Towards the end of 1959, word had reached us in Israel that several documents, again from 'an unknown source' and offered by Bedouins for sale to scholars in Jordan, were in fact found in Nahal Se'elim (Wadi Siyal), south of En-gedi and just north of Masada. Since in the previous survey only the northern part of the Judaean Desert of Israel had been explored, and the area of Nahal Se'elim had remained untouched, the scientific institutions – the Hebrew University, the Israel Exploration Society and the Department of Antiquities – decided once more to send a team out to the region, headed by Aharoni. They spent the week of 25 January–2 February 1960 in the field, assisted again by the Israel Defence Forces. Several caves were examined. Although some interesting finds, including a group of arrows, were made in some of them, it was again clear that the Bedouins had already paid a visit, thus confirming the rumours which had filtered through about the provenance of the newly-found documents. Nevertheless, this expedition managed to detect one tiny cave, very difficult to reach, which seemed to have escaped the Bedouins' eagle eye. Bits of documents were found there and two pieces of phylacteries, apparently of the period of Bar-Kokhba; though one must point out that two coins found in that same cave – one of Elagabalus (AD 218–22) and the other of Severus Alexander (AD 222–35) i.e. about one hundred years after Bar-Kokhba – indicate that this particular cave had been inhabited also at a later period. The results of the team's labour were received by scholars with mixed feelings. On the one hand they showed that even that area, removed from the armistice lines between Israel and Jordan, was prey to Bedouin infiltration; on the other hand one might hopefully still expect occasionally to stumble on a cave that had escaped their scrutiny.

The best defence is attack Several days after these discoveries were made, I happened to meet Mr David Ben-Gurion, then Prime Minister and Minister of Defence, who – when he heard about the recent exploits in the Judaean Desert – expressed concern over the fact that the caves in the Israeli territory of the desert were being ransacked by Jordanian Bedouins undeterred. He therefore ordered the then Chief of Staff, Rav-Aluf Haim Laskov, to increase army patrols in the area. Later that week, Rav-Aluf Laskov asked me a very logical question, typical of his military training: Why be on the defensive? The best defence is, after all, attack! Why, then, be satisfied with sending out patrols to 'defend' the area, rather than launch an all-out archaeological 'offensive' and examine the whole area

thoroughly, once and for all? I accepted this thinking readily
and replied that if the Defence Forces were prepared to assist with
administrative facilities and provide trained climbers for the cliffs,
it was most likely that the archaeological institutions would
welcome the project. The plan was approved by the Minister of

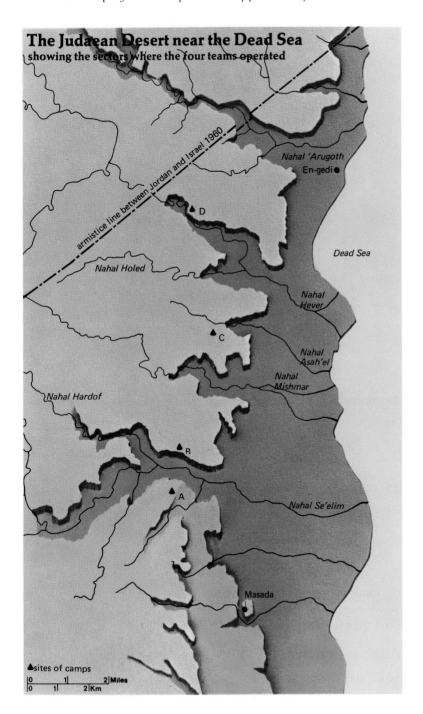

The Judaean Desert near the Dead Sea
showing the sectors where the four teams operated

sector A
the southern bank of Nahal Se'elim; this
canyon is one of the biggest in the Judaean
Desert; its length is about seven kilometres

sector B
the northern bank of Nahal Se'elim and
both banks of Nahal Hardof

sector C
both banks of Nahal Mishmar, Nahal
Asah'el and Nahal Holed, and the southern
bank of Nahal Hever

sector D
the northern bank of Nahal Hever and both
banks of Nahal 'Arugoth; those parts of the
canyons which were within Israeli territory

33

The leaders of the expedition in Beer-Sheva before setting out for the desert: (from left to right) Y. Aharoni, P. Bar-Adon, J. Aviram, N. Avigad and the author

Defence. The amount of material and troops which the army was prepared to supply for the project – in order to cover the very rugged area spread over fourteen kilometres as the crow flies – was enormous; and we knew we would have to recruit the best trained archaeologists available. The army did not wish to extend their help over too long a period, and it was agreed therefore that we would take to the field on 23 March 1960 for about two weeks.

The nature of the terrain determined the method of operation and organisation. The Judaean Desert is a very rugged area, falling abruptly towards the Dead Sea from the eastern slopes of the mountains of Judaea, and is cut by a number of deep ravines, or *wadis*, running roughly from west to east. It is extremely difficult to move in a canyon from one bank to the other without making a detour to the west, and it was clear that it might be impractical to assign one canyon as such to a single team of surveyors; better instead to assign to one team, for example, the southern bank of one canyon and the northern bank of the adjacent canyon. The number of canyons and the means of approach to them suggested that four teams would be the most likely to cover the whole area efficiently; thus it was divided into four sectors, or camps (see map).

The desert divided   Our next problem was to select the heads of the four survey teams. Aharoni was naturally very eager to go, having already spent considerable time in the area earlier. Since the army demanded that the project be concluded within a fortnight, the scientific institutions selected Professor N. Avigad, Mr P. Bar-Adon and

An aerial view of Masada looking north towards En-gedi; the photograph was taken from the helicopter on the first flight to the desert

myself to head the other three teams, although all of us were at that time engaged on other projects. A further meeting took place on 5 March under the chairmanship of Professor B. Mazar, then President of the Hebrew University, to determine the division of sectors among the respective teams. The most coveted sector was naturally Nahal Se'elim, being the least explored and thus the most promising to judge by the recent discoveries. Aharoni was allowed first choice and he selected sector B to enable him to operate mainly on the northern banks of Nahal Se'elim. Professor Avigad then selected sector A, the southern bank of Nahal Se'elim. This left sectors C and D to Bar-Adon and myself and we got them in that order respectively. That no one picked sector D was not because the border with Jordan cut through its canyon (after all at that time the hostile border was near every point in Israel, as illustrated by the then current joke that the train going from Tel-Aviv to Jerusalem had signs reading: 'Do not lean out of the State' . . .), but because Nahal Hever canyon had the least prospects of yielding any finds, having already been thoroughly explored in 1953 and 1955. However, it was decided – to justify the overall effort – to investigate it again. The administration of all four teams was co-ordinated by J. Aviram, the energetic honorary secretary of the Israel Exploration Society.

It so happened that the main discoveries were – contrary to expectation – made in my sector, and therefore in the following pages I shall put the emphasis on the activities of sector D.

In order to be better able to detect the caves, we followed an

The bubble helicopter taking off from En-gedi; from this the first photographs of the caves were taken

unusual course. The caves were mostly in the steep slopes of the canyon banks, and very difficult to discern from the top. Even vertical aerial photographs did not reveal much. The best way seemed to fly by helicopter inside the canyons and photograph the banks at eye level. Helicopters were also required in the preliminary planning of the exact siting of the camps of the various teams. Thus, on 13 March, about ten days before the date set for the start of exploration, the four leaders of the teams were flown by the army in a large helicopter from Beer-Sheva eastwards towards the Judaean Desert. First we hovered over Masada; a really magnificent sight. It was the first time I had seen Masada from the air, and little

The canyon of Nahal 'Arugoth; the southern bank is on the left

did I suspect that three years later I would lead the expedition to this unique site. From there we veered northwards, hopping from one area to another, looking down on the deep and awesome canyons. The site of camp A was fixed on the southern bank of Nahal Se'elim (see map); camp B on the northern bank of the same canyon; and camp C (which also served as the main headquarters for the army and the administration) was put between Nahal Asah'el and Nahal Mishmar right in the middle of sector C. My camp, D, was fixed on the northern bank of Nahal Hever, thus enabling my team to move freely to both parts of the sector, Nahal 'Arugoth in the north, and the northern bank of Nahal Hever in the south. The second objective of flight by helicopter, the actual reconnaissance, was to be achieved in a smaller machine with a transparent 'bubble' cabin, to which we switched on arrival at En-gedi. Each head of team flew the bubble separately in the company of only the pilot and an air-force photographer and surveyed his own sector. I began my flight at Nahal 'Arugoth, a huge canyon with banks rising sometimes almost vertically to about 700–800 metres. We flew at various altitudes, the photographer constantly taking horizontal black-and-white pictures, while I was taking coloured photographs with my Leica. Occasionally, at my request, the pilot would stand the helicopter 'still' to enable us to focus more easily. It was a most interesting experience, though, I must confess, rather a frightening one. The menacing aspect of it was not so much the cliffs and protruding rocks to right and left of us, nor even the 'invisible bank', that armistice border line between Israel and Jordan only seconds away. It was the pilot! From take-off to landing he kept hammering at me with all sorts of questions about Bar-Kokhba: When did he live? What did we know of him? What did we expect to discover now? My timid suggestion that I would answer all his questions on landing safely was to no avail. Only later did I learn from him that not only were some of the manoeuvres he made extremely dangerous and strictly against air-force rules, but, indeed, this was his first flight by helicopter inside a narrow canyon. However, he flew extremely well; in fact he later became commander of the Israel Air Force Helicopter Squadron, and then the Israel Air Attaché in Washington.

After surveying Nahal 'Arugoth we flew in a matter of seconds to Nahal Hever and surveyed and photographed its northern bank which was the southern limit of my sector. This survey by helicopter was of immense importance, although, as we discovered later, it was at the same time very misleading. How smooth the flight and how easy it was to hop from one bank to another! Yet how difficult to get to these same places and descend to them on foot! I returned to Jerusalem rather despondent. The flight by helicopter convinced me – subject to unforeseen surprises in the photographs once they were developed – that I could not expect

overleaf A view of Nahal Hever looking east towards the Dead Sea. The big cave (not seen in the photograph) is in the cliffs on the left

any new caves in my sector, with the exception perhaps of one in Nahal'Arugoth. In Nahal Hever all we saw were the already known and explored caves, particularly the big one under the Roman siege camp. But since the order of the day was to examine meticulously every crevice, nook and cranny, I decided to look even into those caves that had already been thoroughly scrutinised in the past.

Reaching our destination

The remaining ten days were hectic for everybody. The developed photographs were examined carefully and potential caves and crevices marked on the plans with theoretical ways of descent and approach. Special equipment had to be assembled for this unusual expedition: ropes, ladders, torches and lanterns. Joseph Aviram was mainly busy at that time recruiting the labour force for the expedition. Twenty students of the Hebrew University were selected as well as some sixty members of *kibbutzim* (communal settlements) who, together with quite a number of veteran amateur explorers of the previous expeditions, volunteered to join us for that fortnight. Several days before 'D-Day', army units had entered the area and prepared desert paths and tracks. A day before we were scheduled to start, we were informed that our camps were ready on the sites marked and lines of communication established through field telephones between the camps. The area and the army were ready, and so were we!

On the morning of 23 March 1960 the labour force left Jerusalem, and after dividing into the four respective teams in Beer-Sheva, travelled on the dirt track towards the desert. That afternoon heavy rain fell, a rather uncommon occurrence in the desert, but when it does rain it really pours in torrents. Our travel on the dirt tracks was extremely slow and laborious and often quite dangerous, especially along the slopes of the western end of Nahal Hever. From time to time we had to alight from the heavy military lorries and push them along to prevent their sliding backwards. Our advance was very slow indeed, but in due course team A bade us farewell when they had reached their camp, followed by teams B and C, until finally, about eight o'clock at night, we arrived at our destination. It was a tiny camp consisting of small bivouacs. The team numbered sixteen members in all, not counting the soldiers detailed to us, who joined us in our efforts over and above their regular military duties. Needless to say that they preferred these archaeological activities. We arrived, it seemed, in a no-man's-land. All was dark; and we were very happy to be met by Captain Y.Kastel, commander of the reconnaissance unit of the famous veteran Golani Brigade. He was attached to our team and based with us. We appreciated very much indeed the rather meagre but hot army meal that night. After eating we sat down to plan our work for the morrow, Thursday, 24 March, the first day of exploration.

opposite An aerial view of the Roman camp on the northern bank of Nahal Hever

4 Probing

We began with a widespread survey of our section, along the southern bank of Nahal'Arugoth, the cliff face between it and Nahal Hever overlooking the Dead Sea, and the northern bank of Nahal Hever itself. Some of the caves in our sector had already been examined in 1953 and 1955, and our main efforts, therefore, were devoted to the other caves and particularly to those which were visible in the aerial photographs.

Four groups set out to survey the southern bank of Nahal'Arugoth and the eastern cliff face. It did not take them long to find out that most of the depressions in the cliff, visible in the photographs, were no more than crevices and minor cracks. Nevertheless, each such crevice examined, was prominently marked inside with blue chalk to save possible future explorers from superfluous labour. The eastern face was divided into one-mile-wide strips from north to south, and three groups examined those. The results were in the main negative. One or two caves – reached with great difficulty – in which trial trenches were dug, proved to have nothing but animal droppings. In other minor caves a few Roman sherds were found, and occasionally remains of a hearth or pottery of the Chalcolithic period, but no more. (The caves examined are marked by yellow dots on the map.) Possibly a few people did settle in some of these caves for a while, but since the caves were quite small, no Roman guards were posted over them, and it is likely that their inhabitants managed to escape, since the survey teams did not find any skeletal remains there. Other caves in Nahal Hever showed either no remains at all, or traces of Bedouin activity. One by one the groups returned to report their negative results.

While flying the bubble helicopter in the preliminary reconnaissance in Nahal'Arugoth a few weeks earlier, I noticed on its southern cliff – about a hundred metres from the top and one kilometre inside the canyon from its eastern end – a tiny cave, of which the entrance seemed blocked by a huge bird's nest. This cave became known in our jargon as the Cave of the Vulture. I photographed it at that time with my Leica while the pilot made efforts to hover in the air. The study of the photograph and particularly the early reports of the surveying teams indicated that if there was one place worth exploring here, it was the Cave of the Vulture, the least accessible of all and much more so than we anticipated. Although from the top the descent to it seems possible, one discovers after twenty or thirty metres that the rock is sheer vertical cliff almost to the bottom of the canyon. What seemed to

opposite above The tiny opening of the Cave of the Vulture seen through the cockpit of the helicopter and the blurred moustache of the pilot

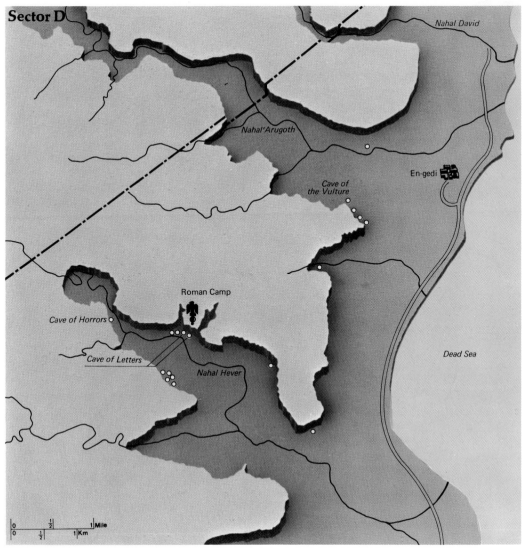

Sector D

Nahal David

Nahal'Arugoth

Cave of
the Vulture

En-gedi

Roman Camp

Cave of Horrors

Cave of Letters

Nahal Hever

Dead Sea

| 0 | ½ | 1 Mile |
| 0 | ½ | 1 Km |

be hopeless did not seem so to the enterprising and courageous Captain Kastel of the reconnaissance unit. At a risk to himself he tried to reach the cave by tying himself to the end of a rope held at its other end by a group of soldiers. Then an idea struck him: why not park a jeep on top near the precipice, then fasten a rope to its axle and a soldier to the other end, and slowly lower the soldier down to the cave. However, since evening was drawing near, we decided to sleep on that idea, and perhaps try it out in the morning. Next day, when Kastel asked for volunteers, the whole unit responded immediately and the first to voice his consent

Tying the rope to the axle of the jeep

was taken. His name was Amatzia (already nicknamed by his friends 'Ometz' – 'courage' in Hebrew). I gave Amatzia some archaeological briefing as to what he should look for. I told him about scrolls, papyri, pottery, etc. Then Amatzia was fastened by paratroopers' harness to the end of the rope tied to the jeep axle and slowly lowered down the precipice, guided from the canyon bed by a soldier with a portable radio. Soon he found himself dangling in the air several hundred metres above the bottom of the canyon and facing the cave, though unable to enter it. It appeared that the rock face at that point was not vertical as we assumed, but concave.

Looking over the cliff as Amatzia was lowered down to the cave

Amatzia did not lose his nerve: he started swinging backwards and forwards like a pendulum, and then picked a good moment and jumped into the cave. A short while later he reported that there was nothing in the cave: no scrolls, no papyri, no pottery, and he added a juicy military curse. He said the opening of the cave was about one and a half metres wide and two metres high, with a depth of ten metres. The inside was filled with rock debris. He dug to a depth of some twenty centimetres, finding nothing but bird droppings. Remembering that the excavators of the caves in Wadi Murabba'at had discovered a papyrus fragment in a bird's nest – which the bird must have picked off the floor – I told Amatzia to search the huge nest and bring up with him whatever was in it. After a while he reported that the mission was completed and so the soldiers began pulling up the rope, but, alas, suddenly the rope got stuck in a crack in the rock and would not give. We did not dare tug at it lest it break. I was very worried and about to ask the army for a rescue helicopter, when Amatzia, full of enterprise and initiative, started climbing up the one hundred metres by gripping the now tight rope in his hands and supporting his feet against the rock, thus pulling himself up slowly and arriving at the top while all of us stood there watching breathlessly. When we saw him walk towards us we forgot all about the disappointing results of the cave and sighed in relief and happiness. Four hours had passed since he entered the cave at 12.30. Looking as if he had just returned from a stroll in a pleasure park, Amatzia came up to me and emptied the contents of his shirt; the outcome was what one would expect from a bird's nest: feathers, straw, bird droppings. However, one item caught our eyes. It bore an inscription. This sudden ray of hope quickly vanished when the inscription turned out to be on a sock bearing the name of a member of Kibbutz En-gedi, a couple of kilometres to the east of us. The bird must have picked this from the *kibbutz* washing line to feather its nest. I have described this episode in some detail, to cool the ardour of any future explorer trying to descend to that cave. I am sure Amatzia was the first human ever to set foot in it. And if any reader has harboured illusions that to discover documents and scrolls all one has to do is hire a cab to the caves near the Dead Sea, I hope our adventures here will dispel them. Thus ended this operation on the only cave in Nahal 'Arugoth of any promise.

The Roman camp

Before embarking on the exploration of the big cave on the northern bank of Nahal Hever – which we quickly became aware might be our only hope – we decided to examine the remains of the Roman camp just above it, which indicated more than anything the importance of those besieged below. Its ruins are merely low walls, built of unhewn stones with dry joints; here and there the upper parts of the walls had collapsed and rubble collected around them. A preliminary air photo enabled us to visualise its

plan, and after some excavation and restoration – which we later carried out – and photography from the air, this plan became very clear indeed. The camp is ideally situated from the military viewpoint and its site was wisely chosen, taking maximum advantage of the local topography to minimise the necessity of building defensive walls, while at the same time providing maximum coverage of the paths leading to, and from, the cave below. Moreover, the existence of a second Roman camp, above the Cave of Horrors, just across the canyon on the southern bank of Nahal Hever, facilitated exchange of information on the activities of the besieged: the camp above our cave could watch the movement of the occupants of the Cave of Horrors and signal it across the *wadi*, and vice

An aerial view of the Roman camp during excavation, looking towards the south-west

47

The Roman camp after excavation and restoration, looking towards the west. In the foreground is the cliff above the big cave

Plan of the Roman camp

1 entrance
2 outer *clavicula*
3 headquarters
4 place of unit standards
5 and 6 main concentration of tents
7 lookout posts
8 store for supplies
9 and 10 hearths

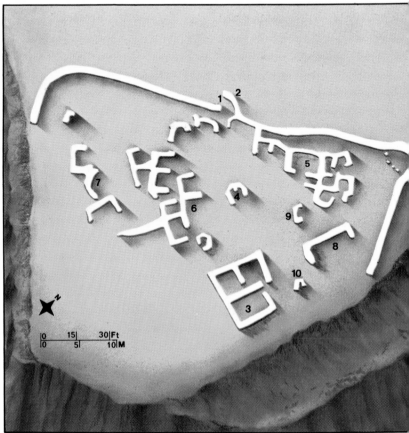

versa. The construction of the camp, close by the precipice, dispensed with the need for a wall on that side. At that spot the land rises somewhat, providing a convenient lookout in all directions, including the depression in the cliff to the west, where, as we soon saw, it was possible to descend to the cave. The main defensive wall runs along the north-west side of the camp, and is about a metre wide and some fifty metres long. At its rounded north-west corner the wall turns ninety degrees and continues in a straight line southwards. In the north-east corner there was a sort of semicircular bastion to provide a means of observation and for flanking fire to the east and north, where the ground is quite uneven. From the bastion the wall turns at a right angle and continues south to the cliff edge. The centre of the northern wall provides the only entrance to the camp, and it is protected by a short wall (*clavicula*). The purpose of the protruding *clavicula* is quite clear: it forms a round tower in the middle of the long northern wall, providing additional means of cross-fire along its eastern section. It is interesting to note that the construction of the *claviculae* outside the wall differs essentially from that of the siege camps at Masada – built sixty years earlier – where they turned inside. In fact our camp resembled more closely the Roman siege camps at Bethar which were its contemporaries. The total camp area is about 1,250 metres square. In its centre remains of small semi-circular constructions were discovered, possibly the place of the unit standards (no. 4 on the plan). In the safer part of the camp, near the precipice, a relatively large structure (no. 3 on the plan) with three rooms was found – undoubtedly the headquarters of the camp. The tents' foundations – remains of which were found inside the camp – show that there were two concentrations of tents, the one (no. 5 on the plan) in the north-eastern section, and the other (no. 6 on the plan) in the western section. The number of enclosures and tents indicates that the camp could hold a unit of 80-100 strong. From the documents which we later discovered, we now know that a *centuria* of the *cohors I miliaria Thracum* was stationed in the En-gedi region till at least AD 124, about ten years before the revolt. Whether or not this unit was destroyed during the revolt (most probably it was), it may be assumed that the two camps beleaguering the caves in Nahal Hever were manned by soldiers belonging to the same cohort, for – as is known from other historical sources – this battalion continued to reside in the Dead Sea area for a considerable time after the revolt. Thus the two camps not only prevented the escape of the besieged from the caves, but the southern camp also cut off the only water supply in the region, the rather rare waterfalls in Nahal Hever, situated to the west of our cave. It was clear from the military position of the camps, without further evidence, that those besieged below could not have escaped or survived.

49

5 The only cave

In preparation for an exploration of the big cave in the northern bank of Nahal Hever, a team of seven – consisting mainly of veterans of the 1953 and 1955 explorations – was sent to improve the approach paths to it. Some of them were reluctant to go and tried to persuade me not to waste more effort on a cave that had been examined twice, counting the Bedouins. However, they performed their duties with much daring and skill. After the second day, when it became apparent that the Cave of the Vulture was empty, our entire team was moved to this cave. And since from now on, you, the reader, like ourselves, will spend some time in the cave, I will first acquaint you with it in detail.

The cave is some one hundred metres below the Roman camp and slightly to the west of it. The canyon's scarp descends vertically from the Roman camp for about ten metres, then slopes off for another fifty metres, after which it again plunges wall-like down to the cave. Eleven or so metres below the cave there is a relatively wide natural ledge. From this down to the canyon bed there is a further drop of two hundred metres. Today – as apparently also in ancient times – the sole means of access to the cave is from the west. There is a recess in the scarp to the west of the Roman camp where the cliff veers slightly to the north, through which the ledge below the cave may be reached. At this recess the slope is not as steep as above the cave, and it is possible, with great care, to climb down using minor footholds in the rock and a 'path' which is often no more than forty centimetres wide. But one wrong step would mean a fall of several hundred metres to the floor of the canyon below. The most difficult, dangerous and crucial passage is upon reaching the altitude of the ledge to its west, at a point where the cliff-face bends to the east. Here the ledge is partially destroyed and its width reduced to one metre at the most. Again, below, there is a nearly sheer drop. Passing through this spot was the real test for all of us, even for those who were not prone to fear of heights. I admit that when I got there for the first time, I hesitated, and were it not for the fact that I was in the lead with others behind me, I would not have advanced. This is not a matter of courage; it is a psychological state of mind. I remember well a brave, courageous major of the engineers who was sent to join us, and having reached that spot, he suddenly became riveted to the ground and could not move. We had to send him back to his unit. So we developed a technique of crossing there: do not look to your right; cling with your body to the rock on your left and just pretend that you are

A dangerous ledge

opposite The big cave with its two entrances and, to the right, a smaller cave. The photograph was taken during the first flight in the bubble helicopter

51

right The narrow ledge leading to the cave, looking towards the west; the man is walking away from the cave
below The sheer cliff-face west of the cave

walking along a narrow pavement that has no plunging canyon
beneath it. However, it turned out that this was just a taste of what
was to follow, in the shape of a vertical cleft in the rock, formed
over hundreds of thousands of years by water rushing down the
cliff face. In the days of Bar-Kokhba passage here may have been
on a narrow ledge of which remains are still visible lower down the
cliff face; but this had since collapsed. The group which was
sent to prepare the way placed an iron bar across the cleft, and this
somehow helped in crossing it. The continuation of the ledge
immediately after the cleft is even more difficult; for here it is not
horizontal, but slopes away from the cliff-face, having been washed
away by flowing water. Here a thick guiding rope was stretched
along, one end fastened near the iron bar and the other near the
crevice in the cliff. It was bad enough to cross it empty-handed;
yet the soldiers and other members of the expedition crossed it
every once in a while carrying the equipment which we needed for
our work. The remainder of the ledge is much better and wider,
and – as mentioned above – it finally passes a point about eleven
metres below the cave. Once there we were faced with the problem
of climbing into the cave proper, so one of the volunteers – like a
mountain goat – climbed the eleven metres of nearly vertical cliff
literally with his fingers and toes. When he reached the top, he
secured one end of a rope ladder to the entrance and had us fasten
the other end with sticks to the ledge below. At that, all of us, like
heroes, followed him up the ladder and into the cave.

Crossing the dangerous crevice on
the way from the cave

Climbing by rope ladder to Entrance 1

Entrance 1 of the cave, looking out towards the south. Note the low ceiling

A horizontal aerial view of the entrances to the cave, and, on the right, the entrance to the adjacent small cave

There are actually two entrances to this cave, some seven metres apart. These are the two openings, or holes, seen on the photograph. We entered through the western opening or, as we shall call it henceforth, Entrance 1.

Darkness and bats

Entrance 1 consists of the actual opening and a long, narrow passage. The opening is rectangular in shape, about eleven metres long and six metres wide on average. The ceiling is rather low and a person of normal stature can just pass through upright. It may be assumed that persons on the look-out for outside movement were posted here, as was indicated later on by some weapons found there. The Bedouins used this place to sort out their finds, and evidence left by them included fragments of cigarette boxes of Jordanian manufacture, bits of English newspapers and pieces of wrapping paper bearing Arabic writing in pencil and ink.

The narrow passage is fourteen metres long and twists and turns. Its ceiling is very low and one has to crawl on hands and knees to get through. The end of the passage is blocked by medium-sized rocks, intentionally placed there to make penetration into the cave proper more difficult. It is therefore impossible to pass directly from the passage into the cave, without climbing over blocks and boulders stacked on top of one another two and half metres high. Beyond them one enters a huge natural hall of irregular shape,

about thirty metres long and eighteen wide in the centre. It is difficult to describe our first impression on entering this hall. Complete darkness engulfed us; thousands of bats flew shrieking past us and rocks littered the floor all around us, looking menacing with their own shadows created by the lights of our torches, lamps and candles. The north-western corner of this hall, hall A, is somewhat rounded, covered with enormous boulders. From this corner a short passage leads to a second hall, B. The passage is two metres long and less than one metre wide, and just half a metre high. To get through it one has to crawl on one's belly. Even those who had no claustrophobic inclinations started feeling rather queasy here. Further on there is another area blocked by natural rock, in which three low, narrow and winding passages exist. Two of these are almost inaccessible, but through the most eastern of the three – a mere half metre in height – one can crawl into hall C, the innermost half of the cave. This chamber is rather long and coneshaped. It measures twenty-six metres in length and its width varies from nine to fifteen metres. Its floor is covered by huge blocks of rock, with hundreds of medium-sized and small stones amongst them.

The entire length of the cave with its three halls, from the entrance to its innermost end, is one hundred and fifty metres.

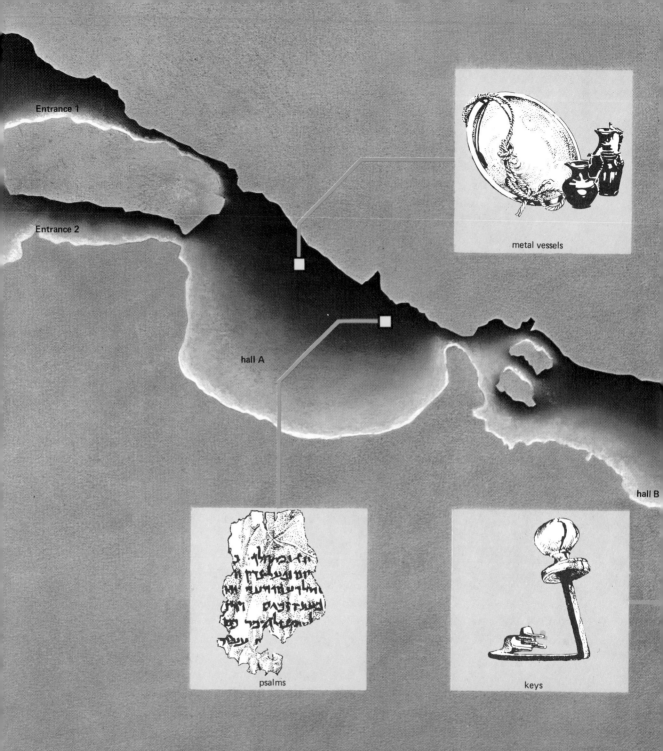

Entrance 1

Entrance 2

hall A

hall B

metal vessels

psalms

keys

The Cave of Letters
showing where the main discoveries were made

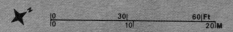

0   30| 60|Ft
0   10| 20|M

Babata archive

glass

net

hall C

passage BB

skulls

Bar-Kokhba letters

6 The niche of skulls

Immovable rocks

The report of the 1953 expedition to this cave was our point of departure. As already mentioned, the most important conclusion reached by that expedition was that the large blocks or rock falls, covering the cave floor, fell from the ceiling *after* the last inhabitants had left the cave. As these blocks are quite immovable and as it was obvious that any use of explosives might cause further rock falls, we decided to ask the Israel Defence Forces for several pneumatic drills with which to break up the blocks in a less violent manner. Transporting the drills and bringing them up the rope ladder was a most difficult task, as was the actual breaking-up of the blocks later; these efforts ultimately proved fruitless, for the lack of oxygen in the cave stifled the combustion of the drills shortly after their activation and the exhaust fumes made breathing – hard enough as it was – virtually impossible. Luckily we determined after only a very short while that the large blocks of rock must have fallen *before* the period of Bar-Kokhba, since many areas of the ceiling were still covered with soot, indicating that there had been no substantial changes in the structure of the cave since ancient times. Therefore there was little sense in trying either to move or to break up these huge blocks of rock, for no level of habitation could possibly lie beneath them.

I still remember with a shudder the suggestion of some of the soldiers to try and widen the passage leading to hall C, with the aid of explosives. We divided the people into groups of twos and threes, and equipped with hurricane lamps, miners' lamps, torches and even candles, they were instructed to examine the many crevices and cavities between the blocks of rocks.

An ugly and terrifying sight

On the second day, Friday, 25 March, while most of my team were still busy with the Cave of the Vulture, a group of twelve started for the big cave and for several hours they transferred equipment: lamps, baskets, picks, and ropes. Only then did they begin to work. One of the volunteers, a real maverick, Pinhas Prutzky of Kibbutz Lahavot Haviva, broke off from the rest and with a candle in his hand decided to survey the innermost hall on his own. Soon enough he rejoined his colleagues pallid and speechless. This state was caused not so much by the fact that he had crawled into a crevice and could hardly extricate himself from it, but rather from the sight which he faced when he got into that crevice. The next day, on my return from project 'Cave of the Vulture', I followed him to his crevice and understood exactly how he must have felt alone there. He led me to the eastern wall of hall C, a

above The crevice in hall C leading
to the niche of the skulls
left Trying to break up large
boulders on the cave floor with
pneumatic drills

couple of metres from the spot where it begins to narrow. I saw there was an opening to a crevice (see the plan of the cave) about half a metre across, between the wall and the adjacent blocks of rock. We crawled along it for two metres, and then the floor began to descend sharply for about a metre, forming a sort of step. Here the passage was most difficult for the height at this point was no more than fifty centimetres, and a largish rock rested on the floor. Only by squeezing and pushing ourselves with difficulty did we at last manage to get in, and found ourselves in a niche, some eight metres long, and about one and a half metres high. To the right of the entrance, above a ledge in the wall, a patch of soot was visible, probably from a lamp that had been placed there in antiquity. Although I had been warned what to expect, I was startled at what I saw once I got used to the dim light. Near the right-hand wall lay a heap of skulls, without their jaw-bones, placed in several baskets stacked on top of one another. At the far end of the niche, in the right-hand corner there was a separate pile of bones and jawbones in baskets and wrapped in cloth between mats. This entire heap had been covered with a large mat. One skull had rolled into

The niche of the skulls with the objects as they were found; on the right are the baskets with skulls and on the left are the mats, clothing and bones

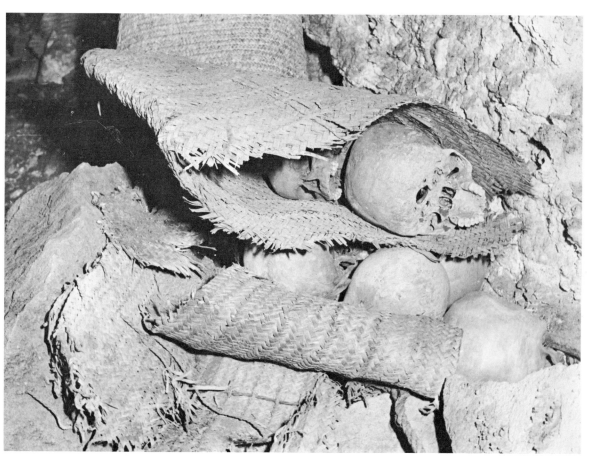

left The first basket with jawless skulls found in the niche
below Other baskets filled with jawless skulls found beneath the first basket

One of the baskets in which
skulls were found

above A close-up of the heap of mats,
clothing and bones as they were
found
right The burial in the floor of the
niche covered by a large coloured
rug (see also page 68)

a crack. In the middle of the niche on the floor were remains of a skeleton covered by a colourful rug and other textiles. Here we found a basket lined in leather, containing the skull and bones of a child wrapped in an almost complete tunic. On the rocks near the left-hand wall fragments of textiles and tufts of hair were found. The skulls and the bones, with the possible exception of those of the burial in the floor, all appeared to have been deposited there at the same time, after having been gathered together, wrapped in mats, and put into baskets.

What was this? we kept asking ourselves. At the time we could only guess what later became clearer: the inhabitants of the cave died of starvation and thirst, but later on, perhaps much later on, their bones were collected, most probably by their relatives or friends, and re-interred in the niche, using the clothes, rugs and mats for shrouds, while the baskets served as containers for lack of coffins. This was our first encounter – as we learned later – with the remains of Bar-Kokhba's warriors and their families. Tragic as the sight was, and despite the fact that no documents were found, that discovery turned out, with further study, to be a mine of information enriching our meagre knowledge of clothing, textiles and mats in the Roman period.

The suffering
of the occupants

The examination of the skulls and the bones, conducted by Dr H. Nathan of the Hebrew University Hadassah Medical Centre, showed them to be the remains of three men, eight women and six children. Later, we discovered some more burials in other places in the cave, but even with these, I do not believe the total number of people who originally came to the cave is represented. It is possible that at one stage – probably before the Romans arrived – some people left the cave and did not return. Whatever the case, it seemed clear that the refugees consisted not only of warriors but also of their families.

What suffering the occupants of the cave experienced in their last phase there, we can only guess. The Jewish Midrashic sources preserve several hair-raising stories about the famine-stricken refugees of the caves, of which some acquire greater credibility in the light of our findings. Thus, in the Midrash on Lamentations:

'It happened to one group who took refuge in a cave. One of them was told: go and fetch a corpse of one of those killed that we may eat. He went forth and found the body of his father and hid it and marked it, and buried it, then returned and said: I did not find any [corpse]. They said: let another go forth. One of them went out, and followed the stench of that corpse and brought it back. They ate it and the teeth of the son became blunt. He asked: whence did you bring that corpse and was answered: from such and such corner. He asked further: what mark was on it? and was answered: such and such mark. He said: Woe to this child; he ate the flesh of his father.'

7 The wardrobe

The textiles

The assortment of textiles discovered was one of the most important finds we made from an archaeological view-point. They are amongst the earliest known of the Roman period and they have one advantage over other finds in that they can be absolutely dated to not later than AD 135. Similar textiles were found in Murabba'at, but not in such good condition and abundance; and some of the textiles found in the Qumran caves, although slightly earlier than ours, are of fewer varieties and types. In addition to the textiles found in this niche, spinning whorls and skeins, or balls, of yarn were in due course found elsewhere in the cave.

These discoveries are a good illustration of the already picturesque words of the Mishna:

'These are works which the wife must perform for her husband: grinding flour, baking bread and washing clothes, and cooking food and giving suck to her child, and making ready his bed, and working in wool. If she brought him one bondwoman [servant], she need not grind or bake or wash. If two, she need not cook or give her child suck; if three, she need not make ready his bed or make wool; if four, she may sit [all day] in a chair. R. Eliezer says: even if she brought him in a hundred bondwomen, he should compel her to work in wool, for idleness leads to unchastity' (Ketuboth v:5).

Dyes and colours

Altogether thirty-four varieties of colours were found. Very good examples of this are the two rugs printed on pages 67 and 68 and the coloured bands on pages 70 and 71 which were achieved by using yarns of various colours. The analysts who examined the dyes for us also admired the way the colours were stabilised and fastened with the most sophisticated mordants of various metal salts, with the help of which the people at this time also succeeded in getting various shades from the same basic dye. Basically only three dyes were used: yellow, red and blue. The yellow is the saffron colour – a dye obtained from the *Crocus sativus* – which was in great demand in antiquity and Pliny mentions that it was often imitated. The red was alizarin, obtained from the roots of *Rubia tinctorium*. According to Pliny again, this was the most important of the red dyes for without it wool stuffs and leather cannot be dyed (*Historia Naturalis* xix: 47). The blue was dyed with indigo, which in various mixtures was one of the most common dyes in antiquity for imitating the famous 'Tyrian purple' (*Murex brandaris*).

The clothing and other woven material showed that the weavers

opposite A coloured rug found with the bones

and wearers of them were very orthodox Jews. Not even once is there an occurrence of mixing diverse kinds of fibres, that is wool and linen or vice versa, as prohibited by the law of Moses. At the same time it was evident that the weaving as such was of very high quality. The most important contribution of these textiles – in addition to what they taught us about techniques in antiquity – was in giving us for the first time a complete set of clothes of the first and second centuries AD, worn by the Jews of Palestine, which, as we shall see, reflect also the fashions throughout the Roman Empire of those days.

Among the woollen textiles there was a large group of rectangular sheets with two parallel bands woven of weft threads differing in colours from those of the web. The bands ran from selvedge to selvedge, with a goodly space between them (pages 70 and 71). Several double sheets were found, i.e. twin sheets – with bands identical in both width and colour – joined together along one selvedge. The section between the bands was left unsewn, forming a slit between the two sheets, which served as the neck opening. Thus was formed a tunic, with two bands running down from the shoulders on both front and back. These tunics are of great interest in several respects: not only are they the oldest tunics of the Roman period to have been found both in a relatively good condition and in a precisely dated context, but they are also the only tunics extant from Mishnaic times known definitely to have been worn by Jews. Hitherto all our knowledge had come from either literary descriptions, or from depictions of clothing in paintings or sculpture. Now we had a good example of the Roman *tunica* which had two bands (*clavi*) descending from the shoulders of the back and the front. Since our tunics have bands of varying widths, maybe they too, like the Roman tunics, designated the rank of the wearer of the garment. We found out later that the people in the cave belonged to the upper classes of local society. This type of tunic, sewn from two separate but identical sheets, is a good illustration of what Varro says about the tunics of the first century BC. In his treatise on the Latin language, this ancient writer has the following to say when he wants to clarify the term *analogia*: 'If anyone were to sew together a tunic so that on one sheet of it the *clavi* were narrow and on the other wide, each would lack *analogy* in its nature.' This description can only fit two-sheet tunics, for the above passage has no meaning with a one-sheet tunic. The latter type was used as well but was less common, and it deserved special mention: 'The soldiers, having crucified Jesus, took possession of his clothes, and divided them into four parts, one for each soldier, leaving out the tunic. The tunic was seamless, woven in one piece throughout; so they said to one another: "We must not tear this; let us toss for it"' (John 19:23–4, The New English Bible). The Mishnaic sources indicate that our type of tunic was the common one,

opposite The large rug, which covered the burial in the niche, after cleaning

Tunics

called *haluq* (its literal meaning 'divided' is thus better understood):
'and so two leaves of a *haluq*, on one of which a defect is visible –
the other is ritually clean' (Nega'im XI:9) or: 'R. Jose said: and the
"opening" of a *haluq* which is made like two leaves' (Palestinian
Talmud, Shabbath 15a). In our tunics the sheets are identical and
so are the bands. Similar to Varro's description, we also have in the
Talmud the following: 'Which is the unskilled and which is the
skilled [tailor]? Said R. Jose ben Haninah: he who matches the
clavi [Hebrew: *'imrah*] is the skilled one and he who does not match
them is the unskilled' (Palestinian Talmud, Mo'ed Qatan 80d).

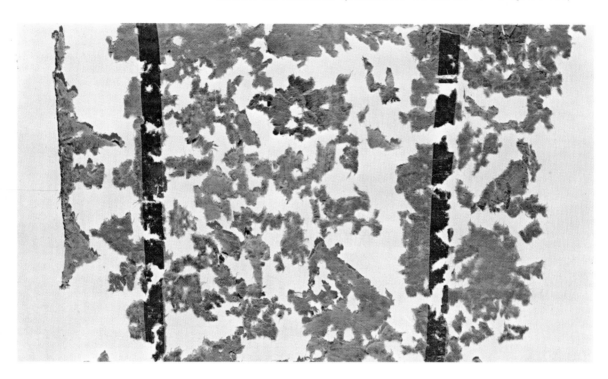

above and right Single sheets of tunic
after cleaning

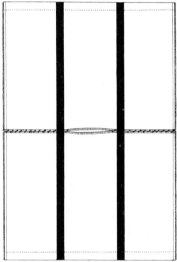

left A tunic found with two of its sheets still sewn together and (*below*) a drawing of the same tunic. Note the slit for the head and the sewing at the selvedges

left A single sheet of tunic of rare colours

Biblical figures depicted in the wall paintings of the Dura Europos synagogue (third century AD) in Syria. Note the bands or *clavi* on the tunics and the notched bands on the mantles. Because of the folds in the mantle only the ends of the notched bands are visible

Part of the notched band on a man's mantle and a drawing of a complete notched band

In addition to the tunics we found a great number of rectangular sheets which have no *clavi* or bands running from selvedge to selvedge, but rather patterns in the shape of bands with notched ends, which begin and end within the web (see below). The identification of these as mantles or outer garments worn over the tunic is proved, *inter alia*, by the depictions on the famous murals from the Jewish synagogue of the third century AD at Dura Europos in Syria, where the men are seen quite clearly wearing mantles like ours with the patterns of notched bands. This type of mantle is like the Roman *pallium* and the Greek *himation*, i.e. rectangular, and thus different from the toga which was semi-circular in shape. Knowing that the wearers were pious Jews, it was surprising not to find on the mantles, or even on the floor of the niche, any traces of the *sisith* (fringe); but this, I believe, is not accidental for, as is evident from Talmudic sources, it was customary to remove the *sisith* from the mantles of persons about to be buried. It is interesting to note the force of tradition from the fact that even the *talithoth* of today are adorned by bands.

In addition to the above mantles we also found a great number of

Women's mantles

A volunteer reading his prayers in the camp; note the bands on his prayer shawl

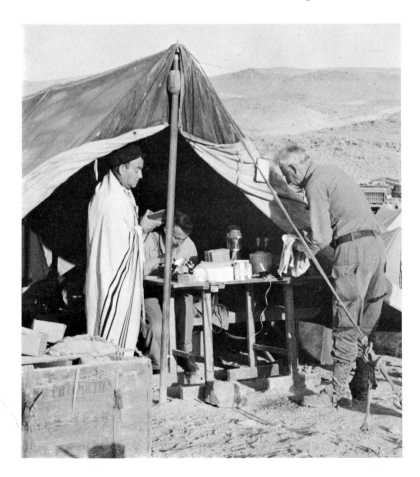

Selvedge patterns and weavers' marks
found on men's mantles

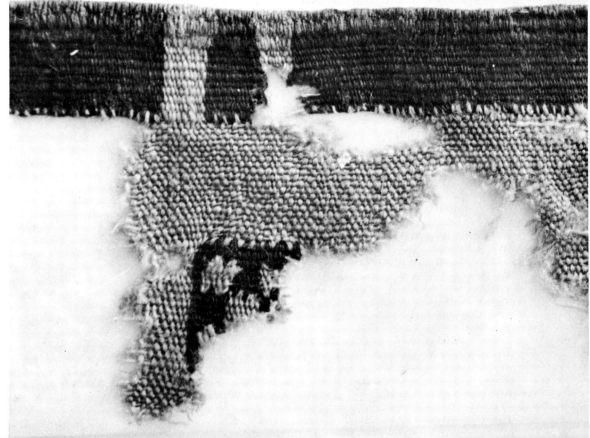

a different type in which – instead of the bands – a right-angle pattern with notched ends similar to the Greek letter *gamma*, adorned each corner of the rectangular sheet. Here, again, the wall paintings of Dura Europos came to our aid, showing quite clearly that the *gamma* patterns appear only on women's garments; the same phenomenon is known from the paintings on several coffins and mummy cases from the first century AD found in Egypt. These show, for instance, that a short notched band appears on the white mantle of a boy, while the *gamma* pattern appears on the mantle of a woman. We are therefore, I believe, safe to assume that our sheets with the *gammas* also belonged to women. An amusing development in early Christian art can now be better explained: in many of the famous mosaics in Rome, Ravenna and Naples, especially

A woman's mantle after cleaning. Note the *gamma* pattern typical of women's mantles

A drawing of the previous mantle showing the position of the *gamma* patterns

A close-up of a *gamma* pattern on a woman's mantle

A drawing of a *gamma* pattern

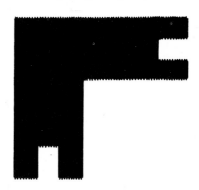

below The infant Moses drawn from the
Nile, as depicted on the wall paintings of
the Dura Europos synagogue. Note the
gamma patterns on the women's clothes
right and bottom Lids of painted
Egyptian mummys' coffins of the
Graeco-Roman period. Note the
notched bands on the boy's mantle
over the banded tunic and the *gamma*
patterns on the woman's mantle

from the fifth century AD and later, one can see that all the mantles of Biblical figures are depicted with a single pattern similar to the Greek letter *gamma*. It is known that Christian artists used earlier Jewish illustrations and particularly illuminated Bibles in order to emulate their motifs. By that time the differences between the two types of mantles had been forgotten, and as the *gammas* appeared in full while the notched bands were partially concealed in the garment's folds, they may have assumed that all the patterns were *gammas* and shown their important figures in the mosaics wearing women's garments. Because these patterns resemble letters and especially the *gamma*, they were referred to in Byzantine literature as 'gammadia'. The pattern ultimately became the most popular in the altar-cloth of the Christian Church and even the altar-cloth itself came to be known as *gammadia*.

Another most interesting find was a child's linen shirt or tunic,

An early Christian mosaic of Jesus and his disciples from Ravenna (fifth century AD), showing the misuse of the *gamma* pattern on men's mantles

of which parts were tightly tied by string to hold, bag-like, various items such as herbs, spices, and seeds. Since the tunic belongs to a very small child, it may be assumed that the 'bags' and their contents were of a prophylactic and curative nature. This type of tunic, too, is referred to in the Talmud, in the typical manner when the oral authorities for any statement are quoted in full. The Mishna in Shabbath VI:9 says: 'Children may go out with bindings and princes with bells'; to this the Gemara adds: 'what are bindings [*Qesharim*]? Said Adda Mari, in the name of R. Nahman ben Barukh, in the name of R. Ashi ben Abin, in Rab Judah's name: *Qesharim* of madder [*Rubia tinctorium*]. Abaye said, mother told me three *Qesharim* arrest [illness before it starts]; five cure it; seven are effective even against the witch-craft' (Babylonian Talmud, Shabbath 66b).

Later, and elsewhere in the cave, we found a bundle of wool, wrapped in a piece of wool mantle, which although dyed was still

opposite A child's linen shirt as it was found. Note the small 'bags' tightly tied by string to hold such items as herbs, spices and seeds

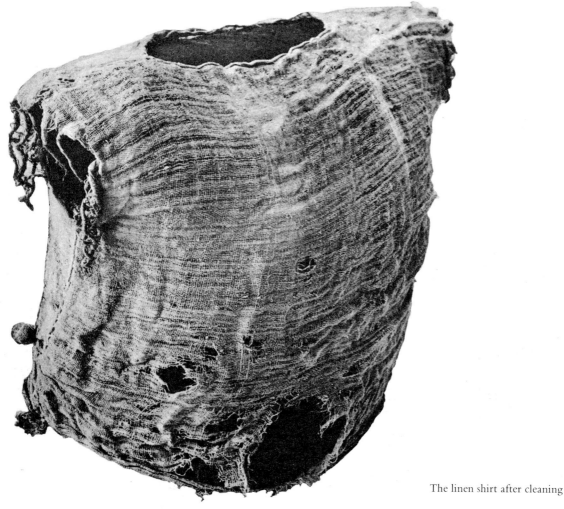

The linen shirt after cleaning

81

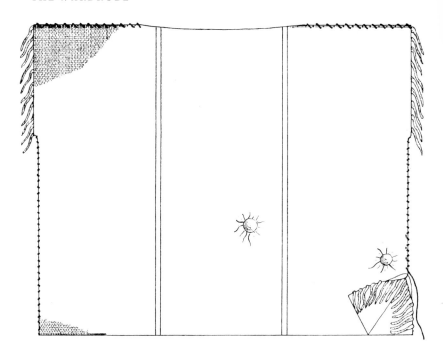

A drawing of one sheet of the linen shirt showing the position of the 'bags'. The shirt was made of two identical sheets sewn together along the selvedge in the manner of the tunics

Some of the contents of the 'bags'; among the objects shown here are a shell, salt crystals, seeds and several objects of unidentified materials

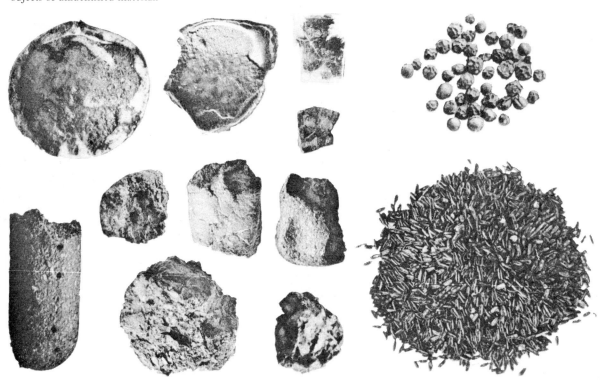

unspun. With it we found several unfinished ritual fringes (or *sisioth*). The colour of this dyed wool was identical with that of the Tyrian purple (obtained from *Murex brandaris*) believed by many to be the Biblical *Tkheleth*, the colour of the *sisith*. However, an analysis by Edelstein and Abrahams of the Dexter Chemical Corporation of New York showed that the colour of our fringes was not obtained from *Murex brandaris*, but rather from indigo and carminic acid. (Carminic acid is the colour principle of the well-known kermes dye, obtained from the female of the insect *Coccus*

Bundles of wool, dyed in 'purple' but still unspun, found in the cave

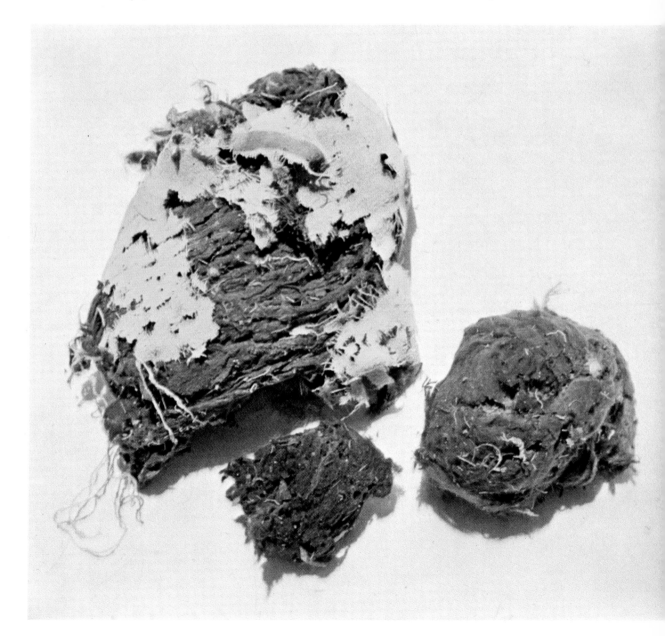

ilicis which lives on a particular species of oak [*Quercus coccifera*] and is even today considered very precious.) This offered us a chance to learn very important facts about the problems of the true *Tkheleth* which confronted pious Jews, and were of great concern to the rabbis. In disturbed times, as those of Bar-Kokhba, it was most difficult to obtain this expensive dye and it was thus often imitated and faked. Since in practice it was almost impossible to tell the real *Tkheleth* from the imitation, the rabbis ruled: 'There is no manner of testing the *Tkheleth*; it should therefore be bought only from an expert' (Babylonian Talmud, Menahot 42b). Some makeshift tests, the Talmud records, were actually confusing. How a bundle of wool, such as ours, dyed not with Tyrian purple but – as ascertained by Edelstein and Abrahams through infra-red spectro-photometry – with indigo, kermes and highly sophisticated mordants which gave it the appearance of true purple, would stand up under these tests, is unknown. Let us, at least, give the people of the cave the benefit of the doubt, that they bought it *bona fide* from a non-expert, unaware that it was an imitation. According to the Talmud (Babylonian Talmud, Baba Metzia 61b): 'It is I who will exact vengeance from him who attached to his garments threads dyed with indigo and maintains that it is *Tkheleth*.' In other words, the real crime was when the fake was deliberate.

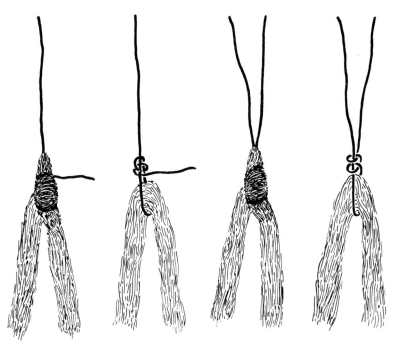

left Partially completed ritual fringes
found within the unspun wool (*opposite*)
above A drawing showing the technique
by which the fringes were made

8 The clue of the coin

After the discovery of the niche with the skulls, work proceeded in all parts of the cave with little success, but the fact that a niche had been discovered, which to all appearances had not been detected by the Bedouins, was encouraging and our spirits rose. Our main problem was the maintenance of the hurricane lamps which, affected by the diminishing oxygen in the cave, kept going out, until a special member of the team, Menahem Magen, was detailed to supervise them. We named him 'Prince of Lights'. Prince or no prince, he was subject to the same standing orders binding all members of the team, that bodily functions would be performed outside the cave, on the extreme end of the ledge. So, on Tuesday, 29 March, four days after the discovery of the skulls and garments, Magen went out to the ledge for that purpose. On his way back, but while still on the ledge not far away from the rope ladder, he found a coin with the inscription 'Shimeon' on one side and 'of the Freedom of Jerusalem' on the other. The coin may have fallen from the entrance above, either during the occupation of the cave, or possibly the Bedouins had found it and lost it again when leaving the cave. When the coin was discovered, one of the soldiers asked me what it was worth. I replied that that type was common enough and could be bought cheaply from any antiquities' dealer, but when found here in the cave it became priceless. This was our first indication that this cave had actually been occupied in Bar-Kokhba's time. It so happened that indirectly it led to one of the most important discoveries we made in the cave. The Commanding Officer of Southern Command, Aluf Avraham Yaffe, who happened to visit us after the coin was found, suggested that a mine detector be employed in search of further coins. Meanwhile, the find of this one coin prompted a more intensive search of Entrance 1, which had been almost completely cleared by the Bedouins and the 1953 expedition. In the eastern corner of the entrance an arrow was found with the upper part of its wooden shaft still attached to it. It was of the common type found in Murabba'at and the other caves, and two other arrows like it were subsequently found in Entrance 2 of our cave. Probably they belonged to guards posted at these entrances to watch the cave's approaches.

'Let there be light'

The electric generator which we requested from the army arrived on Thursday, 31 March, and the soldiers installed it near the Roman camp, whence a cable was rolled down to the cave's entrance. It was a technical feat. On Friday, after several delays and hitches, the

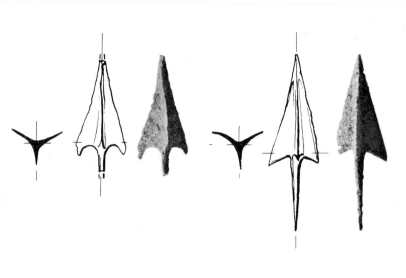

below The author and members of
the team examining the arrow found
in Entrance 1; the arrow had part of
its wooden shaft attached to it

above and right Drawings and photographs of the arrow found in
Entrance 1 and the two arrow heads
found in Entrance 2

electric network was in operation and an additional cable was fixed along the cave inside, with light bulbs attached to it at intervals. It is difficult to describe our feeling when the first bulbs went on. All at once the dark cave became less menacing and the working conditions were completely transformed: for suddenly we could see what we were doing, and movement over the blocks of rock became free. 'The cave is lit up by electricity for the first time in two thousand years,' someone joked. We did not relieve the Prince of Lights of his duties; his task was now to ensure the burning of lamps in various corners of the cave, in case the electricity should fail. To be trapped in darkness in the innermost part of the cave was a frightening possibility.

That same morning we began to use the mine detector which arrived the preceding day. Two soldiers operated the instrument, while some students followed them, prodding the earth wherever something seemed 'suspicious'. First we subjected the ledge outside the cave to the detector, then Entrance 1, and finally hall A.

Working with the mine detector in Entrance 1

89

This operation was conducted light-heartedly by the soldiers as they knew that there was no danger of treading on a mine, and they kept joking about the crazy archaeologists. A short while later, while I was engaged in hall C, I saw Prutzky rushing towards me calling me to come to hall A. On my way there he told me that at a distance of ten metres from the entrance, near the western wall, the needle of the mine detector began to quiver and a persistent and continuous buzz indicated the presence of metal. I arrived to find great commotion: the mine detector was buzzing, surrounded by a number of excited onlookers, but no metal objects were in sight. 'Maybe the buzz is caused by our working tools?' ventured one of the soldiers logically. So we removed all tools from the vicinity and even took off our hobnailed boots. Still the buzz continued unabated. We decided to start digging.

The discovery of the basket after it had been located by the mine detector; masks were used as protection against dust and stench, and a 'puffer' was used to blow dust off the objects

The basket after the objects had been removed   91

It so happened that that morning the three photographers, all freelancers, who were attached to the expedition and moved between sectors, arrived at our cave with all their gear, including a heavy movie camera, which they dragged up the ladder with much difficulty. They were rather desperate; for a whole week they had been wandering from camp to camp without anything spectacular to photograph. They had by then photographed every tent, every truck, every volunteer, every canyon, but no finds. They were alerted to the buzz, and like vultures over a cadaver they arrayed themselves around us, ready to shoot.

A basket   Tension was high as we started to excavate. The bat-droppings gave off an unbearable dust and odour and several of the diggers resorted to dust-masks. A medium-sized stone was removed and when digging had gone on for another fifteen centimetres, suddenly a basket came into view, lying on its side. 'The army has given us a basket detector,' remarked someone, but no one paid attention to his joke. As I began to lift the basket, one of the soldiers said: 'Beware, it may be a mine!' and automatically I hesitated for a fraction of a second. The atmosphere of the cave had a strange effect and somehow one tended to react irrationally. The mine

The basket before opening;
its handles were tied together with a
rope which was also attached to the
large bowl

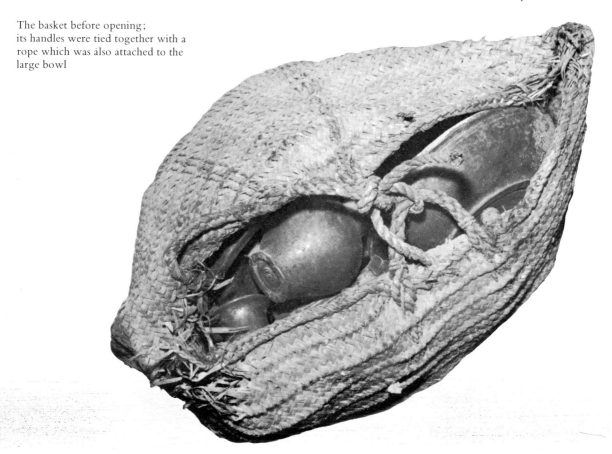

detector was lowered to the basket and the buzzing became more audible. When I turned the heavy basket over, a spontaneous cry of delight and astonishment escaped everybody's lips. Between the tightly tied handles of the basket we could clearly make out a number of bronze vessels.

We paused briefly to make arrangements for proper registration of the finds, and then I untied the handles and we could see many strangely shaped objects. It was really difficult to believe that so many vessels were packed into that one basket. The colour pictures overleaf, although taken later in Jerusalem, were done before the objects were cleaned with just the dust brushed off them. They show all of the nineteen objects that this basket contained.

The following facts were noted immediately: the palm-frond rope which tied the handles together at one end was fastened at the other end to the handle of a very large bowl inside the basket, in which there was another smaller bowl. Both of them were placed vertically on one side of the basket; on the other side, again vertically, were a *patera* (a pan-like vessel) and three shovels. Between them we could see a number of jugs.

The bronze vessels

The basket after opening with the objects *in situ*

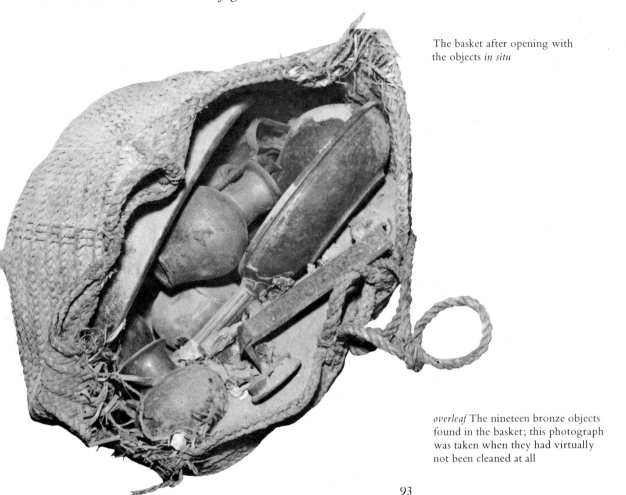

overleaf The nineteen bronze objects found in the basket; this photograph was taken when they had virtually not been cleaned at all

93

The large bowl with the rope
attached to its handle; the rope is
made of palm-frond fibres

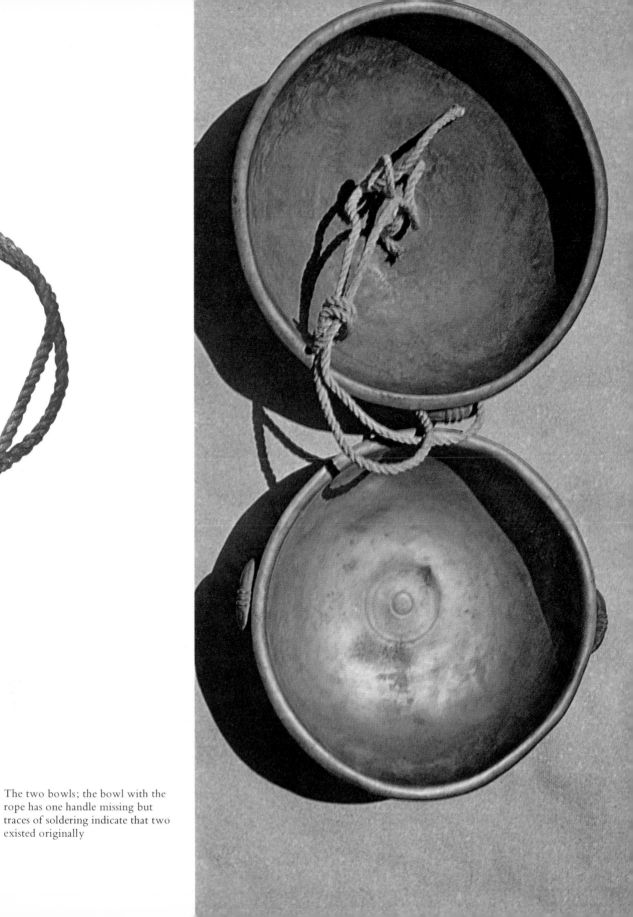

The two bowls; the bowl with the
rope has one handle missing but
traces of soldering indicate that two
existed originally

At last the photographers also had their field day. Every phase and movement of ours was recorded in stills and movies. The terrible dust which blurred some of the pictures only added to the authenticity. The resulting movie is one of the few genuine and unedited documentary films of an archaeological discovery-in-the-making that I know of. I took out the objects one by one, acting to the onlookers the role of a magician with his rabbits. Out came twelve jugs, then three shovels, then the beautiful *patera*, then the key, and lastly the two large bowls: altogether nineteen objects.

While the first excitement over the strange set of objects died down somewhat, questions and thoughts crossed my mind: these objects looked old, Roman, definitely pagan in nature; was it

overleaf Four of the twelve jugs found in the basket

A photograph (*opposite*) and drawings of the second bowl. The drawings indicate that the bowl's base was turned by lathe. Note the eagle-like heads at the end of the handles under the bowl rim

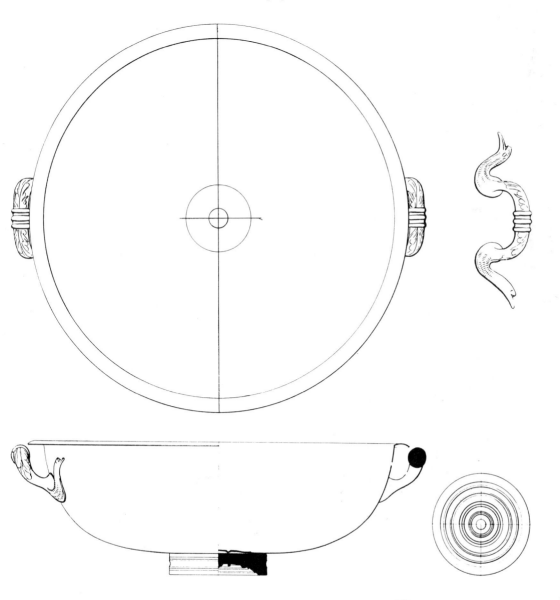

Examining the defaced image on the bottom of a jug handle immediately after its discovery

possible that they belonged to the orthodox fighters of Bar-Kokhba? Could a *patera* bearing a medallion clearly taken from Greek mythology belong to these Zealots? Were the jugs, depicting deities at the bottom of their handles, used by Jews? A closer look made me notice that the images of the deities were defaced; on one of them we could easily see marks of filing; sometimes the images were totally erased, and sometimes partially so with only the tips of their noses affected. This indicated that the objects, although originally pagan, became usable by Jews through this partial effacing of the pagan images. The many Mishnaic rulings in this connection are not only confirmation of such a theoretic possibility, but proof that such defacing was in fact practised in the time of the Second Temple and Bar-Kokhba: partial or symbolic effacing, if only of the nose, was sufficient to allow such vessels to be used: 'How is an idol desecrated? If a gentile cut off the tip of its ear, or the end of its nose, or the tip of its finger, or battered it even though naught was broken off, he has desecrated it' (Abodah Zarah IV:5). Thus we had for the first time archaeological proof of that practice as it was performed. Many of the vessels were originally cultic in nature and it is quite possible that the people of Bar-Kokhba took them as booty from one of the Roman units or temples in the area.

opposite A detail of the defaced jug handle and drawings of the jug. Note the file marks on the defaced image

102

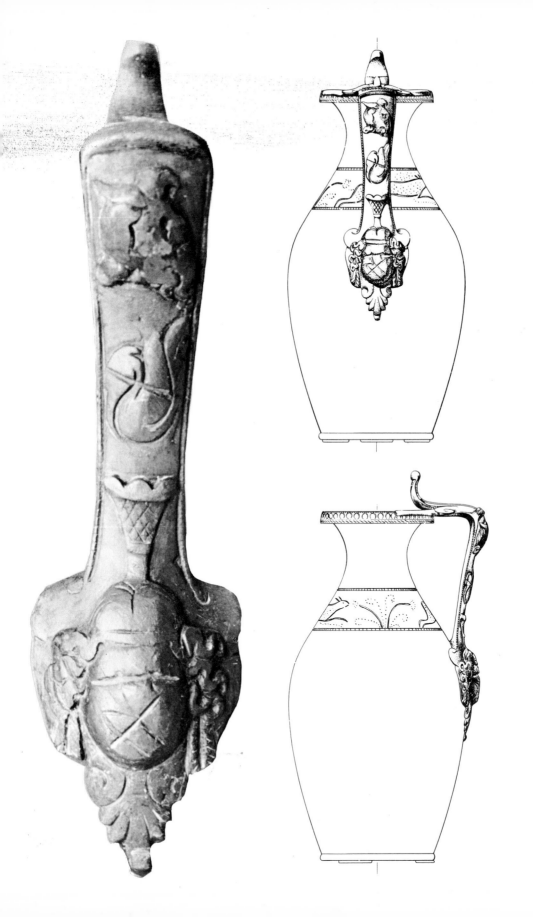

When the study of these objects was later completed in Jerusalem, it became quite clear that the discovery of the bronze vessels was of importance from a general archaeological view-point: they were absolutely dated and their state of preservation was superb because of the dry condition of the cave. It became evident that the objects not only were of Roman origin but were most probably manufactured in Capua, one of the famous metal-producing centres in Italy. Quite a number of exact parallels were found in Pompeii and Herculaneum, dated in the latter part of the first century A D. The enormous quantity of objects of superb artistic merit discovered there is responsible for the fact that the relatively less elaborate objects, like ours, were rarely considered worthy of scientific publication. During the summer of 1960 I visited the museums of Pompeii, Herculaneum and Naples and was fascinated by their many unpublished vessels, almost identical to ours.

The patera

The *patera* is the most pagan in character and at the same time the most beautifully made of the objects we discovered. It consists of two parts soldered together: the cast-and-turned bowl and the cast handle. The diameter of the bowl, including the rim, is 22.6 centimetres. The handle is fourteen centimetres long; it is hollow and shaped like a fluted column terminating in a ram's head. The centre of the bowl has a medallion encircled by a 'beads' pattern, eight centimetres in diameter. It consists of a scene from Greek mythology: Thetis, the mother of Achilles, rides on a sea-centaur, bringing weapons to her son. The centaur has a human upper body, an animal lower body and a fish's tail. Thetis rides the centaur with her body facing forward, her feet turned left, and her head to the right. Her right leg is crossed under her left. The upper part of her body is nude, while her back and abdomen are wrapped in a mantle. In her left hand she holds a sort of mace or spear and in her right something resembling a helmet, or shield. The faces of both the centaur and Thetis had been intentionally defaced, until little more than the eye sockets remain. It is generally agreed that such *paterae* were used for libation; in fact, in some Roman reliefs, one can see a *patera* upon a Roman altar. Although *paterae* of this type in general are quite common in Pompeii and Herculaneum, those bearing medallions are rather rare. I know of about five. A very similar *patera* from Pompeii is now in the British Museum. There too, the subject of the medallion is taken from Greek mythology: Scylla destroying the companions of Odysseus; the faces have not, of course, been obliterated or deliberately defaced.

One similar *patera* came to my attention in strange circumstances and I shall recount this episode here as a warning to those who buy antiquities without proper advance checking. In 1961 I was invited to see a private collection in London. To my amazement I saw there a *patera*, very much like ours, but with a different medallion. When

The discovery of the *patera*; *paterae* such as this are thought to have been used for libation

The *patera*; its handle terminates in the shape of a ram's head

A side view and drawings of the *patera*

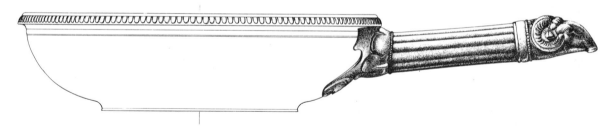

106

I asked the owner where the *patera* had come from, I received the astonished reply: 'Why, this was discovered by you in the Bar-Kokhba caves!' It turned out that the owner purchased the *patera* at a well-known saleroom in London; in the catalogue the *patera* was described as having been excavated by me in a cave near the Dead Sea and as belonging to the booty taken from the Romans by the Bar-Kokhba insurgents. At my request the owner referred the matter to the saleroom who, on 28 December 1961, replied in writing: 'It was announced at the time of the sale, when you were present, that the note given below this lot covering its provenance referred to another identical object [i.e. the *patera* we discovered in the cave]. This amended statement was on view in the saleroom, and an announcement was made verbally at the time by the auctioneer.'

The medallion in the centre of the *patera*; it shows Thetis, the mother of Achilles, riding on a sea-centaur (*triton*) and bringing weapons to her son

The three incense shovels were of special importance particularly because of their fine state of preservation and because certain details have been preserved which are generally lacking in shovels from other sites. The largest of the three and the most ornate of them is unique in its decoration and state of preservation. It measures thirteen by seventeen centimetres and its handle is eighteen centimetres long. It consists of four elements: the pan, the cups, the handle and the legs. Of particular interest are the cups which are, as far as I know, the only example of such cups preserved intact. It seems that the coals themselves were placed in the pan, while the cups served to hold various kinds of incense, sprinkled from time to time over the coals. The shape of such shovels is depicted in Jewish art of the Roman and Byzantine period. Together with the *menorah*, the *lulav* and the *ethrog*, synagogue mosaics quite often depict the shovel, Roman style like ours, to represent the incense shovel of the Temple.

The incense shovel

Drawings of the large shovel. The two incense cups, still intact, make this shovel unique

Details of a jug showing part of its handle with a defaced image, the base and the view from above. These details are basically typical of all the jugs found in the basket
opposite Another jug with a defaced image on the handle

Some of the jugs too were originally made for libation; this is particularly evident from the wine jug with the trefoil rim. Of interest are the handles, most of which bear some decorative motif, usually at the bottom, where we find a human mask or the face of deities. These in particular were subject to erasing and defacing by the Bar-Kokhba people. All handles terminate in two arms embracing the rim and soldered to it, thus joining the handle to the jug. The most popular motif for the arms is the neck and head of a bird.

It became clear that all these objects were deliberately packed and hidden underground. This indicated that the inhabitants of the cave at one time contemplated escape, and must have hidden their treasures in preparation for it. As we know now, their chance never came.

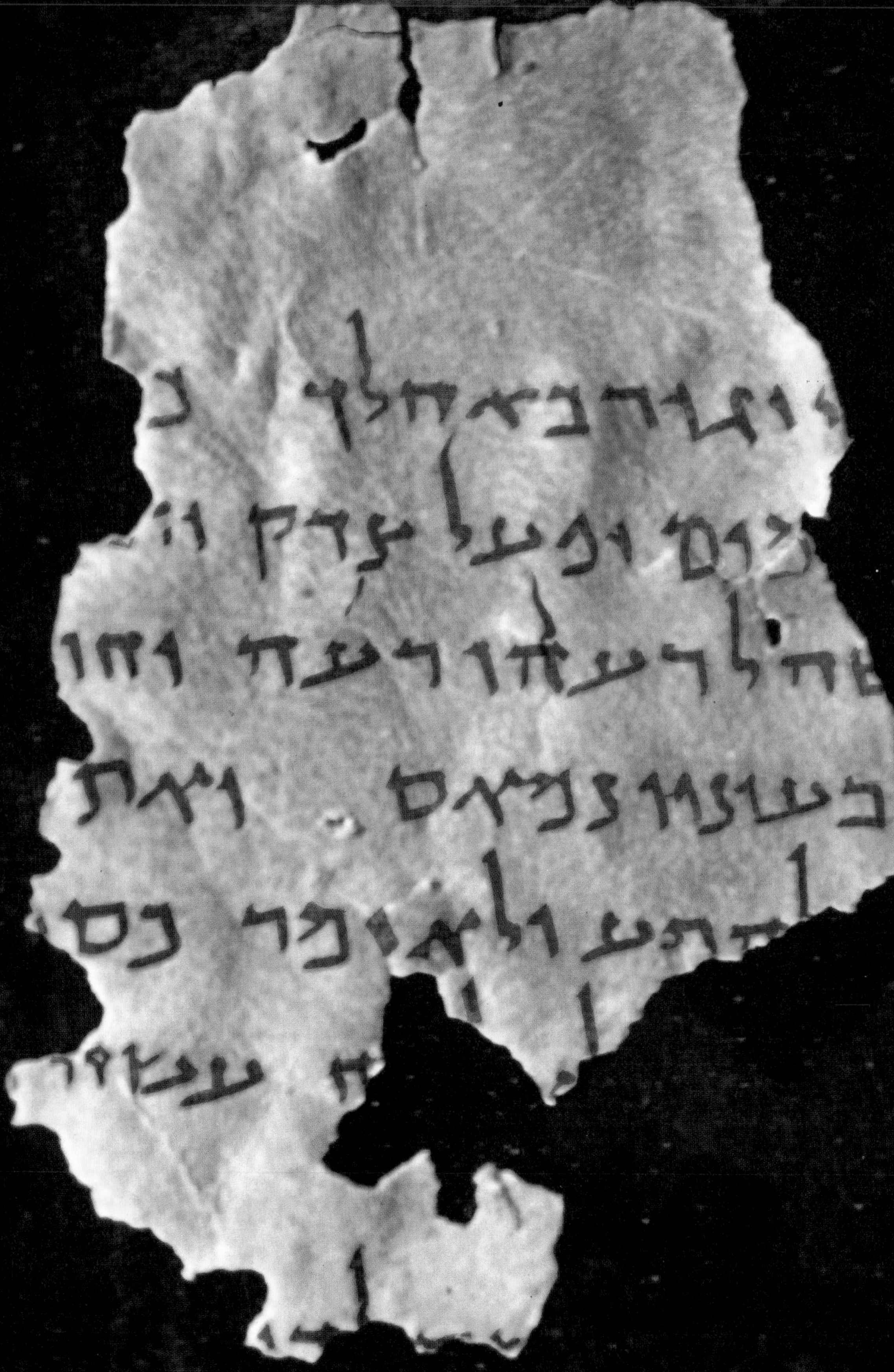

וֹ

וֹיזרח בעחלן ב

ום ויעל יצרק וו

חל רשעה רשעה והן

בשעת ציבס ויזת

תש ויזמר בס

עבאו

9 The great find

On Sunday, 3 April – having spent the previous day, the Sabbath, bathing in the wonderfully cool springs of the oasis of En-gedi – we resumed work energetically. Everyone felt convinced that great discoveries lay ahead of us. The find of the metal objects induced us to clear all the heavy boulders and stones on the left side of the cave – between the place of that find and the passage leading to hall B – and dig up a strip two metres wide. This task was bestowed on a group of soldiers who had joined us that day. In my trunk, back at the camp, I had been keeping two bottles of brandy and I told the soldiers that whoever discovered the first written document, irrespective of its size, would get one of the bottles as a prize. (Another object I kept in my trunk was a heavy concordance of the Bible, but that I kept in secret lest I be ridiculed for my expectations.) One of the soldiers, who was removing heavy boulders in the front hall, hall A, was a unique fellow. He was Solomon Bakri, a relatively new immigrant from North Africa, and settled in Moshav Yoshivyahu in the Negev: a strong, husky, red-headed boy, known to all his friends as Ginger. He had terrific physical strength and could move very heavy rocks single-handed. But that, perhaps, was not uncommon. He also knew the Bible by heart. Even this may not have been uncommon; the unique thing was the combination of the two. In his own primitive and naive way he loved stories about the history of the Jewish people. When he saw the discovered skulls, he could not believe they had belonged to the warriors of Bar-Kokhba. 'It is impossible,' he said. 'The size of these skulls is exactly like mine; yet the Bar-Kokhba warriors were heroes, they must have been giants with much bigger skulls.' Ginger worked like a giant: he was determined to find a written document.

A short while after work began on that memorable Sunday, Ginger – who was working close by where the vessels had been found – uttered a shout. I was somewhat irritated and short-temperedly said to him: 'Ginger, you'd better keep your shouts till you find some scrolls.' He said nothing but ran towards me and in his trembling outstretched hand there was a fragment of a scroll. I started to read the writing: 'O Lord, who shall sojourn in thy tents' and 'He who walks blamelessly, and does what is right,' when Ginger immediately joined in, saying 'Psalms' and simultaneously with the Prince of Lights, added 'Chapter Fifteen!' There was no need for my concordance: they were absolutely right. Pandemonium broke loose. At last here was a written document,

A fragment of a scroll

opposite The fragment of the Psalms scroll containing verses from Chapter Fifteen and the beginning of Sixteen

113

albeit only a fragment! I believe that there was no happier person on earth at that moment than Ginger. I gave him the bottle of brandy. As he was a teetotaller he passed it on to his friends, but he kept the empty bottle as a souvenir and asked me to autograph it. I can still see his shining eyes as I write these lines. Alas, Ginger is no more; he was killed in the Six-Day War of 1967. He fought gallantly and I am sure he visualised himself as a descendant of the Bar-Kokhba warriors.

The fragment of the parchment contained several lines written by a trained hand. It was one of the earliest well-dated fragments of Psalms known at that time, and contained verses from Chapters Fifteen and the beginning of Sixteen. The scribe had left a blank space between the two, which shows that the division between the chapters then was identical with our division today. Since the Psalm is written in parallel verses separated by a narrow space, it is easy to assess that the width of the written portion of the page was seven and a half centimetres. Accordingly, the text can be reconstructed.

The text and spelling are identical with the Massoretic (i.e. traditional), except for the omission at the beginning of verse three of the words: 'Who does not slander with his tongue.' As the fragment was found near the passage leading from hall A to hall B, we may assume that it actually belonged to a scroll found by the Bedouins and was torn off when they crawled out. For confirmation of such a possibility we will have to wait until the documents from an 'unknown source' are published in their entirety.

A water skin   On the previous Wednesday some new volunteers joined our team. Among them was a perfect trio from the *kibbutzim* south of Mount Carmel: Rami Mines was the born leader; Yoram Vites was the nosey type, the explorer; and Haim Liphshitz was the good-natured fellow with the sense of humour. They worked as a team and on the Sunday they asked to be transferred to the innermost hall C. They were 'fed up' they said, with the prosaic work of removing stones in hall A; they had heard about the niche with the skulls and wanted permission to explore its vicinity. As in any case I was planning to re-examine that hall now that we had electricity, I gave them permission to go ahead. So off they went, equipped with an extension cable with bulbs, which could be connected at various junctions to the main cable running along the centre of hall C. The news about the discovery of the Psalms fragment had by that time reached the other teams of the expedition and I was expecting the visit of Joseph Aviram and other colleagues around lunchtime. Shortly before their arrival, while I was still busy in hall A, Haim of the trio came up to me, his usual smiling mien looking quite serious. He uttered only two words: 'Come along.' Obediently I followed him to the innermost part of hall C where I saw Rami near the lights but could not see Yoram.

'What is the matter?' I asked. Rami replied that this could best be explained by Yoram.

'But where is he?'

'There!' he said and pointed to a crevice between the wall of the cave and the large boulder on which he was leaning. I tried to squeeze in after Yoram but it was not easy and I had to push parts of my body in with my own hands. About three metres below I saw Yoram, his body contracted and folded in a slit measuring no more than about eighty centimetres square. I shone the bulb towards him and realised that he could hardly move. At his feet was a big bundle of leather, which later on proved to be a water skin

top The water skin made of goat hide after cleaning and partial restoration

bottom Various objects of a cosmetic nature found in the water skin: a silver earring, wooden powder box, bone handle, ladle and glass cosmetic oil container

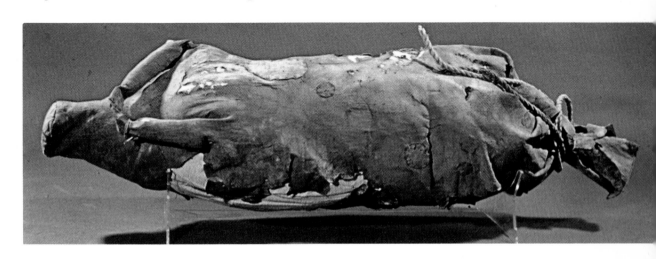

made of goat hide. Seams were visible but it was torn in the middle and all of Yoram's efforts to push it upwards were futile. The crevice opening was too narrow to pass the torn bag, which according to Yoram was full of 'things'. We decided therefore to empty the objects through the tear. Yoram handed the objects to me one by one: I passed them on to Haim, who passed them on to Rami, who in turn put them separately into empty buckets. As I was working I could hear, high above me, the excited voice of Aviram who had arrived and was leaning on top of the crevice. Chips of stone and loose earth rolled on my head, but down there, in the depth of the crack, it felt as if the cave walls were collapsing on me. I begged them, therefore, to stand away from the opening

below right The torn water skin as it was found and a detail of the water skin showing the original patches sewn over natural holes – such as the navel and anus – in the belly of the goat hide

above Skeins of wool found in the water skin

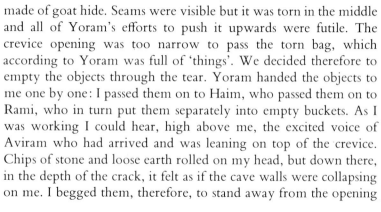

and promised to give them a running commentary.

The first objects to emerge out of the water skin were balls of wool, varying in colours, still intact. A woman's bag, no doubt! The next objects strengthened this thought: all sorts of beads, cosmetic tools, perfume flasks, and lastly a mirror, which lay by the water skin. Woman's nature seemingly has not changed in the last two thousand years; here was one who knew she was entering a dark cave, but nevertheless she did not fail to bring her mirror along. And what a strange mirror! A shining brass disc in a case made of two pieces of wood in the shape of table-tennis bats. More objects kept coming out: a baby's tunic, a bundle of dyed, unspun wool, rags, fragments of garments and other pieces of textiles.

A bundle of papyri!

Some of the jewellery found in the water skin: the silver earring (two views) and beads of semi-precious stones such as carnelian, agate, amethyst, quartz, blue glass and sardonyx

above The mirror found near the water skin. The mirror disc is made of brass and is held in a wooden case, the two halves of which are shaped like table-tennis bats
right Drawings of the mirror showing technical details including the exterior of the case which is overlaid with red parchment
opposite A glass jug found near the water skin, after restoration

The bundle of papyri as found; note the careful folding of the papyri, the strings with which the bundle was tied together and the slats of wood with writing on them

What made that woman bother to hide this stuff in the most remote end of the cave? At that moment Yoram handed me a bundle tied by string. 'Look!' he said. I stared at a bundle of papyri, folded, tucked together and tied by one thick and one thin string. Between the papyri I could even detect thin slats of wood with some writing on them. They were all carefully packed and, as they seemed very fragile, I decided to touch the papyri as little as possible until we got back to Jerusalem. What could this bundle be? The fact that it was found in a woman's bag probably meant that the documents were very precious to the woman. Was it her marriage contract? Or perhaps formulae against evil spirits? At that time I did not dare voice my wishful thoughts.

The remaining two days, until we packed and returned to Jerusalem on Wednesday morning, were somewhat of an anti-climax, except for one short moment. On Monday, while we were

having our light lunch in the cave entrance, Sheraga, a soldier of
the Engineer Corps, approached me pale as a sheet and said: 'I
discovered rows and rows of jars full of scrolls!' Then he ran back
with all of us running after him. We got to passage BB, that long
passage projecting from hall B. Two-thirds inside and on its left
Sheraga pointed to a crevice. 'There, inside,' he said. He had found
a niche. We looked inside and saw skeletons wrapped in mats and
a basket with two skulls. 'Where are the scrolls?' I asked. He seemed
dazed. It turned out to be pure hallucination, in which the skulls
looked like jars to him. Later he told me, embarrassed, that the
previous night he had dreamt that he was going to discover scrolls.
However, the new niche with burials – similar to the one we had
already discovered – was interesting in itself, and we patted him on
the back in consolation. We had no cause to complain and returned
to Jerusalem with a rich harvest.

Next day, at home, I rose late, and immediately tried to get in touch with Professor G. Bieberkraut. Bieberkraut came to Palestine from Germany before the creation of the State of Israel; he was an artist and a restorer of old paintings. In 1948, during the siege of Jerusalem, it was he who unrolled the first three Dead Sea Scrolls acquired by my late father, Professor E. L. Sukenik. He also un-rolled one of the four scrolls which I purchased in 1954 in the USA.

I telephoned him now, but there was no reply from his home. So, impatiently, I opened the box in which I kept the bundle of papyri and began to examine it closely for the first time since its discovery. I did not dare touch the papyri themselves, but I managed carefully to pull out of the bundle two of the four wooden slats which I had observed already in the cave. The other two were still folded inside the bundle. The two I took out had clear letters in ink, in cursive writing of the type discovered at Murabba'at. I copied the letters on to a piece of paper, one by one. My hand copied automatically without my mind registering the words. When I finally looked at what I had scribbled, I could not believe my eyes. It read: 'Shimeon bar Kosiba, President over Israel'! I rushed to my wife Carmella and told her. 'Are you sure or is this another hallucination?' she said, having heard from me the previous evening of the episode with Sheraga. 'I will check with Professor Avigad,' I said. Avigad, my colleague, head of team B in our expedition, is a noted epigraphist. I traced the letters exactly on a fresh piece of paper and took it over to him without comment. He looked at it very carefully for several minutes, then looked back at me with shining eyes. We embraced each other silently.

The beginning of the wooden letter. It reads 'Shimeon bar Kosiba, President over Israel' (first line) 'to Yehonathan and Masabala, peace. [My order is] that you search' (second line) 'and seize the wheat which is in the possession of Hanun [or Tahnun]' (third line)

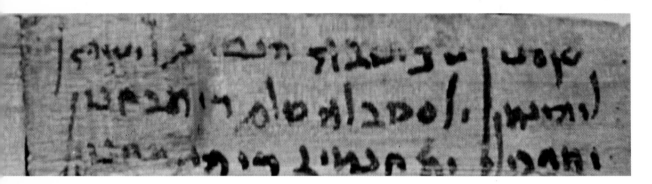

The following morning I went to Bieberkraut. I showed him the bundle of papyri without telling him anything about their contents and enquired when he could start the process of unrolling and photographing them, the latter being done by Mrs Bieberkraut. It came as a hard blow to learn that they were planning to spend Passover with friends outside Jerusalem, as was their custom every year. This meant that they could start working only eight or nine days later. I did not wish to press the eighty-one-year-old man, knowing how he and his wife looked forward to their holiday. I also suspected that he must be thinking that what had waited in a cave for two thousand years could not be all that urgent. . . . They promised me at least to extricate the remaining two wooden slats from the bundle, see if the four fitted together, and photograph them before they went on holiday. This they did. Indeed, the four slats fitted together to form a rectangular piece of wood seventeen by seven centimetres. I studied the document for a few days; it turned out to be a letter from Shimeon bar Kosiba to two people named Yehonathan and Masabala, names that meant nothing to me at that time.

After Passover, Bieberkraut returned and started to work. He had to be extremely careful. The papyri were very brittle and as they were folded several times, there was always the danger that they might break off at the fold, as some did. A few days later Bieberkraut called me and said that four documents were ready for me. I rushed over and saw immediately that all of them started with the name of Bar Kosiba and all were letters. Slowly but surely, the rest of the bundle was unrolled. It consisted of fifteen letters, or despatches, some of them extremely well preserved and some of them less so.

I worked feverishly, day and night, to decipher the writing. It was not easy because many of the documents were written very cursively, but I wanted to know the contents of each of them to be ready with my report for the gathering at the President's home. It is difficult to describe the reaction of the people gathered on that occasion, and indeed the emotion of the whole country, when the news was released. Newspapers came out with gigantic banners and leading articles, and everyone was elated. Obviously this was not received as just another archaeological discovery. It was the retrieval of part of the nation's lost heritage.

10 The letters speak

General comments
on the letters

The letters are the most personal and direct evidence concerning Bar-Kokhba and his relations with his subordinates. At the same time they are a mine of linguistic data. The best way to describe them is to let them speak for themselves.

The first thing that struck us was that for no apparent reason some of the letters were written in Aramaic and some in Hebrew. Jews at that period were versed in both languages, yet since most of the letters were in Aramaic, possibly Hebrew had just lately been revived by a Bar-Kokhba decree. I remember that when I showed the letters to Mr Ben-Gurion, then the Prime Minister, only the Aramaic documents had as yet been opened. 'Why did they write in Aramaic and not in Hebrew?' was his immediate angry reaction, as if the scribes had been members of his staff.

It is interesting to note that despite the fact that the letters are written in the first person singular by Shimeon, no two letters bear the same handwriting, so they must have been dictated in an over-staffed office. . . . In some of the letters it is indicated that the scribe was so-and-so son of so-and-so. Not one letter is signed by Shimeon bar Kosiba personally.

Only the 'wooden' letter, mentioned earlier, has the title: 'President over Israel'; the other letters begin simply: 'from Shimeon ben/bar Kosiba', once more a confirmation that Bar-Kokhba's real name was Ben Kosiba, a fact already ascertained from the Murabba'at letters (see Chapter 2). Actually his name was written KSBA, without the vowels, as is the custom in Aramaic and Hebrew. It was only from one of the Greek letters that we learned that his name was pronounced *Kosiba*.

The letters are addressed to one, or both, of the following persons: Yehonathan son of Be'aya and Masabala son of Shimeon. These two were apparently the military commanders of En-gedi. Fortunately one of the letters actually refers to them as the 'Engedites'. It is quite clear from the contents of the letters that they were sent by Bar-Kokhba to Yehonathan and Masabala before these men escaped into the caves.

If style is any criterion by which to judge men's character, then Bar-Kokhba seems to have been a strong and tough man, not unlike his description in the Jewish sources. The letters are written in an abrupt – even telegraphic – style. Most demands and orders are coupled with an admonition. Maybe it is unfair to pass the above judgement, since clearly these letters were written towards the end of the revolt, when Bar-Kokhba was already desperate.

Let us now review the best preserved letters. We begin with the four slats of wood. When opened and fitted together, they formed one piece, which – since it was too big to be packed with the other papyri – had been broken into four. In one place there is an X mark, written by a later hand, indicating where the joint should be. The writing is in two columns, from right to left. An incision was made down the back, to facilitate the folding, and it thus formed what the Greeks called a *pinax*. The practice of writing on wood was widespread in the Orient and is often mentioned even in rabbinical literature. The letter itself, written in Aramaic (with some Hebraisms), begins thus: 'Shimeon bar Kosiba, Prince over Israel, to Yehonathan and Masabala, peace.' Yehonathan – whose father's name was Be'aya (or Be'ayan in its Aramaic form) – must have been the senior of the two, since the letters when not addressed to both are addressed to him alone. Masabala is a rather rare name; Josephus mentions one Masabala, father of the priest Hanan, who was killed by Shimeon bar Giora in the First Revolt. The Talmudic literature retains a tradition concerning a tax-collector by this name. Our Masabala could well have belonged to the same family. From other documents to be mentioned later on, we know that Masabala (whose father's name was Shimeon) was involved in some of the land transactions which took place in En-gedi. The letter deals with several subjects in this order:

a) The confiscation of a quantity of wheat belonging to one Tanhum (or Hanun) son of Yishma'el, and its transfer in safe custody to Bar-Kokhba. Interestingly, the letter employs the Greek word *asfaleia* for safe custody, a term which is preserved only once in rabbinical literature. Bar-Kokhba threatens to punish Yehonathan and Masabala should they fail to carry out the order: 'And if you do not accordingly you shall be punished severely.' The man himself is also to be sent to him in *asfaleia*.

b) A severe warning not to give shelter to any man from Tekoa: Tekoa, a Biblical city (the birth-place of the prophet Amos), is situated near Bethlehem, on the fringe of the Judaean Desert, in the direction of En-gedi. Some of the wealthier citizens of this city were known from the times of Nehemiah as evaders of national duties (Nehemiah 3:5). Now, apparently, some of the Tekoans were disregarding the mobilisation orders of Bar-Kokhba, and were seeking refuge in the somewhat remote En-gedi. The warning and the punishment threatened were quite severe as became clear to me only recently when this passage was correctly interpreted: 'Concerning every man of Tekoa who will be found at your place – the houses in which they dwell will be burned and you [too] will be punished.' This subject must have bothered Bar-Kokhba more than once, since another Aramaic letter – a papyrus of twenty-four by ten centimetres, with eight lines of writing – reads as follows:

'You shall be punished severely'

'Shimeon Bar Kosiba to Yehonathan
and to Masabala . . . let all
men from Tekoa and other places
who are with you, be sent to me
without delay. And if
you shall not send them, let it
be known to you, that you will
be punished. . . .'

En-gedi, being far away from the battlefront, was a natural haven for shirkers and Yehonathan and Masabala were apparently accused of giving them shelter.

c) The arrest of Yeshua bar Tadmoraya: the order proceeds to decree: 'And seize Yeshua bar Tadmoraya [= the Palmyrenian?] and send him to me in safe custody.' Who was this Yeshua? We do not know, but most probably he was an officer: 'and do not neglect to take off his sword'. The letter is signed by a certain Shmuel bar 'Ami.

A call for help

In a short letter, written on a long papyrus (twenty-one by nine centimetres) which is rather difficult to decipher in its entirety, Bar-Kokhba asks for reinforcements: 'Shimeon bar Kosiba to Yehonathan son of Be'ayan and to Masabala . . . get hold of the young men [or: servants] and come with them; if not – a punishment. And I shall deal with the Romans.' This is the only document of Bar-Kokhba in which the Romans are so designated. Normally they are referred to as the 'gentiles'. The order proceeds with a demand that Yehonathan and Masabala bring with them a certain Thyrsis son of Tinianus (or Theodoros) 'since we need him'. Thyrsis was apparently a non-Jew who may have co-operated with the forces of Bar-Kokhba. Or the reference may, of course, be to a man who was captured. The letter ends with the usual greeting 'Be well' (literally: Be in peace).

opposite above A papyrus letter beginning 'Letter of Shimeon bar Kosiba, peace. To Yehonathan bar Be'aya.' It deals with an unspecified mission of a certain Elisha

opposite below The top of a letter ordering Eleazar bar Hitta to be sent to Bar-Kokhba before the Sabbath

En-gedi, the only village in Bar-Kokhba's realm situated on the shores of the Dead Sea, is the subject of a very simple request written informally in Aramaic by a crude hand: 'From Shimeon to Yehonathan and Masabala, peace! . . . send to the camp four [donkey] loads of salt. . . .'

A secret mission

In another short letter (in Aramaic) but written by a very trained scribe, we read the following:

'Letter of Shimeon bar Kosiba, peace!
To Yehonathan son of Be'aya [my order is] that
  whatever Elisha
Tells you do to him and help
him and those with him [or: in every action].
Be well.'

The subject of this letter, addressed only to Yehonathan, was

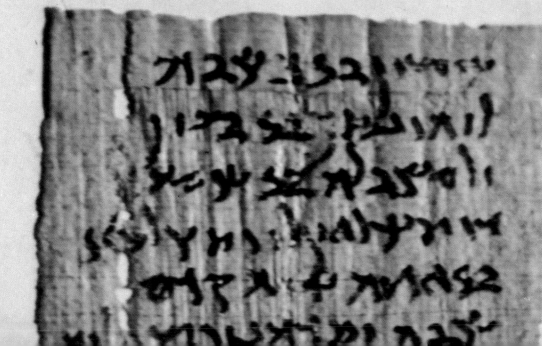

apparently confidential, but Elisha (whoever he may have been) was authorised to transmit it by word of mouth to Yehonathan. Incidentally, this is the only letter which actually begins with the word 'letter'.

Eleazar bar Hitta

One of the most interesting orders dealing with an important citizen of En-gedi, is again written in Aramaic, on a medium-sized papyrus (twelve by seven centimetres). The letter is preserved in its entirety, and it contains thirteen short lines, which, in typical Bar-Kokhba style, deal with the arrest and confiscation of property of a certain Eleazar bar Hitta (see picture on page 127):

> 'Shimeon bar Kosiba
> to Yehonathan bar Be'ayan
> and to Masabala bar Shimeon
> [my order is] that you will send to me Eleazar
> bar Hitta immediately, before
> the Sabbath [or: the end of the week].'

This Eleazar became known to us later from other documents discovered as a wealthy landowner in En-gedi (see Chapters 12 and 16). Apparently he did not co-operate whole-heartedly with Bar-Kokhba. The order goes on to specify what should be done with his property: 'The wheat and fruit should be confiscated and if anyone oppose you, send him to me and I shall punish him.' Yehonathan and Masabala are ordered to see that the herds should not trample and destroy the trees; then again a warning of 'a severe punishment' and finally: 'and as for the spice orchard, let no one get anywhere near it'! At the end there is the following signature: 'Shimeon bar Yehudah has written this,' obviously the scribe. The particular order to protect the 'spice orchard' is of great importance. En-gedi was renowned for its various spices, particularly the balsam shrub. Its quality was so well known that according to Pliny in *Historia Naturalis*, when the Romans conquered En-gedi in the First Revolt, they had to fight over every shrub against the Jews who wanted to destroy them and deprive the Romans of these precious spices.

The 'four kinds'

We come now to one of the most interesting letters in Aramaic consisting of five long lines (the papyrus is twenty-two by six centimetres). It deals with a request by Bar-Kokhba to supply him with the 'four kinds' – the *lulav* (palm branch), *ethrog* (citron), *hadas* (myrtle) and *arava* (willow) – required for the feast of Succoth (the feast of booths or tabernacles). The pathetic nature of the request lies in the fact that it is made in the midst of the war (or more probably towards its end) and Bar-Kokhba goes into great trouble to get them. It is also a testimony to Bar-Kokhba's strict religious piety. There are many problems concerning this letter, so it might be best to present it as it is and then single out the main points:

128

1 'Shimeon to Yehudah bar Menashe to Qiryath 'Arab(v)aya I
have sent to you two donkeys that you shall send

2 with them two men to Yehonathan bar Be'ayan and to Masabala
in order that they shall pack

3 and send to the camp, towards you, palm branches [*lulavin*] and
citrons [*ethrogin*]. And you, from your place, send others

4 who will bring you myrtles [*hadasin*] and willows [*aravin*]. See
that they are tithed [literally: set in order] and send them to
the camp.

5 (the request is made) since the army is big [in Aramaic: *bdyl dy
'okhlesa sgy*]. Be well.'

This is the only letter of Bar-Kokhba not addressed to Yehonathan and Masabala, but to a person unknown to us named Yehudah
son of Menashe, who dwells in Qiryath 'Aravaya. Bar-Kokhba is
sending him two donkeys to take two people to Yehonathan and
Masabala who, as we know, were in En-gedi. They are to load the
donkeys with palm branches and citrons (for which En-gedi was
famous) and send these towards Yehudah. Bar-Kokhba also
orders Yehudah to send other men to the surrounding area of
Qiryath 'Aravaya for myrtles and willows – for which the area is
presumably known. It is interesting that Bar-Kokhba gives specific
orders to Yehudah to 'set [the citrons] in order'. 'Setting in order'
is a common expression in Talmudic literature, referring to setting
aside the tithe. Bar-Kokhba wants to receive the donkeys' load of
citrons after tithing 'since the army is big', i.e. he needs quite a lot!
That Bar-Kokhba specifically orders them to be tithed, indicates
that he does not trust Yehonathan and Masabala, who must have
been considered '*am ha-'ares* (literally: people of the land; a
rabbinic usage to designate unlearned people not to be relied upon
to keep to the letter of the law).

The fact that Bar-Kokhba himself had to send the donkeys from
his camp to carry the 'four kinds' indicates the inadequate transport
at the disposal of his subordinates. It also reflects the measure of his
uncertainty as to whether his orders would be carried out unless he
sent the necessary transport.

The letter of the 'four kinds' in
which Bar Kokhba requests palm
branches, citrons, myrtles and
willows – the 'four kinds' needed
for the feast of Succoth – to be
sent to him

Where was
Qiryath 'Aravaya?

The inclusion of this letter in the bundle kept by Yehonathan and Masabala may be explained thus: when Yehudah sent the donkeys, he sent the letter along as confirmation of Bar-Kokhba's order, and the letter remained in the possession of those in En-gedi. Yehudah's post – Qiryath 'Aravaya – was obviously situated between Bar-Kokhba's main camp (Bethar?) and En-gedi. But where exactly? The name Qiryath 'Aravaya is otherwise unknown. Its literal meaning is 'the town [or village] of the Arabs ['*Arvaya*]', or, more probably, in the light of the contents of the letter, 'of the willows ['*Aravaya*]'. A possible key to the location of this site lies perhaps in a most intriguing legend preserved in the Midrash on Lamentations 1:15 (which is full of stories concerning the two revolts). According to this legend, a certain man from Judaea (or: a Jew) was ploughing his field and his cow lowed. An Arab (or as we may now think a man from 'Arvaya) passed by and told him to set free his bullock and plough because the Temple had been destroyed. When the cow lowed a second time, he told him to harness his bullock and plough for the King Messiah had been born. When the ploughman asked the name and birth-place, he was told that the name was Menahem ben Hezekiah, and the birth-place was 'the fort (or town) of 'Arva of Bethlehem in Judah'. The site of this place was identified by scholars with a ruin – 'Arib – near a village rich in springs and orchards which lies on the main route between Bethar and En-gedi, north-west of Tekoa. Another possible site to fit that description could, in my opinion, be 'Arub, – a village between Bethlehem and Hebron – in which very recently caves had been found with objects from the Bar-Kokhba period, including coins. The letter was written on the eve of the Succoth feast, and we may assume that the date was the autumn of AD 134, since by Succoth of 135 (around September) – if we are to accept the Jewish tradition – Bar-Kokhba was no longer alive.

'Written in Greek'

Another letter – obviously connected with the request for the 'four kinds' – is one of the two Greek letters found in the bundle. It sheds further light on the above episode; but its main interest lies in the additional information it gives us on the composition of the Bar-Kokhba army.

The letter is addressed to Yehonathan (son of) Be'ayan and Masabala, yet the sender is not Bar-Kokhba but someone else, whose name is unfortunately not well preserved: So . . . ios, most probably not a Jew. S–s informs Yehonathan and Masabala that he is sending them a certain Agrippas, so that they should send back with him palm branches and citrons 'for the camp of the Jews'. He urges them to be 'as quick as possible – do not do otherwise'. Then comes a surprise: 'the letter is written in Greek as we have no one who knows Hebrew [or Aramaic]' and he could not delay writing it 'because of the holiday'. The letter concludes again with the warning 'Do not do otherwise' and the usual 'Be well'.

The Greek letter which also requests the 'four kinds' for Bar-Kokhba. The letter was sent from an intermediate camp and it explains that it is written in Greek 'as we have no one who knows Hebrew'

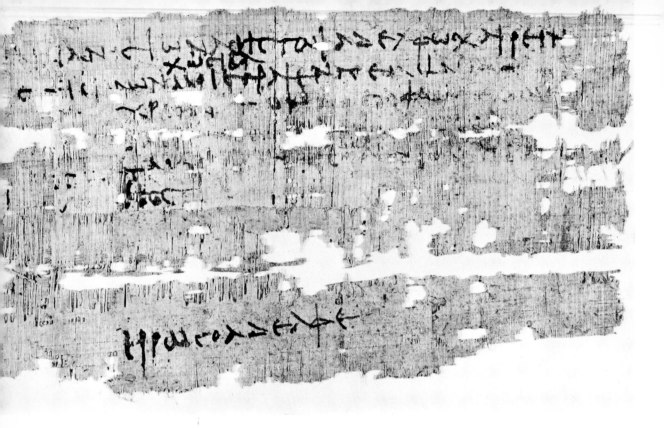

A Greek letter with Bar-Kokhba's name: 'Simon Khosiba'. Note the insertion of the word *xwsiba* above the line

Simon Khosiba and Ailianos

Yehudah bar Menashe was seemingly not around when the previous letter arrived, and a member of his staff hastened to forward it to Yehonathan and Masabala with a covering note. The sender was probably a non-Jew. This is indicated by the language of the letter, and particularly by his use of the phrase 'camp of the Jews' to refer to Bar-Kokhba's camp – a usage which was perhaps common among the non-Jewish members of Bar-Kokhba's army. The existence of gentiles in the Bar-Kokhba ranks is further corroborated by Dio Cassius's hostile words: 'And many outside nations [i.e. non-Jews] were joining for eagerness of gain.'

An unexpected confirmation comes from the second Greek letter. This letter is badly preserved, but what remains is of considerable interest. It is the only document found with Bar-Kokhba's name preserved in Greek, thus: 'Ailianos to Yonathes the brother, greetings. Simon Khosiba has written to me that you must send the . . . for the needs of the brothers . . . [Ailia]nos. Be well, my brother!'

Several points merit elaboration. The sender of the letter is a non-Jew, as his name implies: Ailianos in Greek is equivalent to the Latin Aelianus. This name was quite common from the days of Trajan and Hadrian (Publius Aelius Hadrianus). Ironically our Aelianus collaborates with the rebels. Aelianus began by writing just 'Simon' and then added 'Khosiba' on top of it for further identification, since 'Simon' was quite a common name. Here we learn for the first time that Shimeon's patronym was pronounced with an i: *Kosiba*. Like the writer of the previous letter, Aelianus too was stationed somewhere between Bar-Kokhba's camp and En-gedi, most probably in the same Qiryath 'Aravaya. It is a pity that the nature of goods requested is obliterated, but apparently he too refers to the same request for citrons and palm branches which Yehonathan and Masabala, it seems, were not so quick in supplying. Lastly, an interesting point emerging from this letter is that the Bar-Kokhba fighters used to refer to each other as 'brothers', a usage not uncommon in revolutionary movements. The same appellation is also used by Bar-Kokhba himself in the last letter to be discussed, the most touching of all.

A large (nineteen by nine centimetres), badly-preserved papyrus is one of the few letters written in Hebrew; it is also perhaps the most indicative of Bar-Kokhba's desperate situation at the end of the revolt. This letter concerns the cargo of a ship in the port of En-gedi, with which Yehonathan and Masabala did not deal properly. The letter begins:

'You care nothing for your brothers'

> 'From Shimeon bar Kosiba to the men of En-gedi
> To Masabala and to Yehonathan bar Be'ayan, peace. In
> comfort you sit, eat and drink from the property of
> the House of Israel, and care nothing for your brothers.'

What a touching and tragic note is in these words, written by the failing Prince of Israel!

Found with the letters was a tiny piece of clay, bearing a seal impression and with a bit of string still clinging to it, which had originally bound the folded papyrus. This impressed clay served – like wax nowadays – to seal off the letter and had a dual purpose: to prevent its opening by the 'postman' and to guarantee its authenticity – the seal of the sender being known to the receiver. The interest in our seal impression is mainly its motif: a bearded man in a short tunic, struggling with a lion standing on his hind-legs and grasping the man with his forelegs. Although this motif was quite common in Graeco-Roman *intaglios* representing Hercules killing the Nemean lion, in the Bar-Kokhba headquarters it might have symbolised the struggle against Rome. The design and figures on the impression are in relief (*cameo*), which means that the

The seal

A Hebrew letter to 'the men of En-gedi', Yehonathan and Masabala, discussed on this page

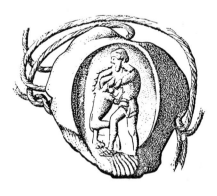

above The seal impression with string found with the letters (scale 1:1) and an enlarged drawing of the impression. It originally sealed one of the letters

The other culprit – Yeshua ben Galgoula

right A side view of the bundle of letters, as they were found
opposite A letter found in Wadi Murabba'at from the administrators of Beth Mashkho to Yeshua ben Galgoula. Note the signatures

actual seal, or ring, bore a design in *intaglio*. According to some rabbis this was permissible despite the injunction against 'graven images', to quote the following: 'A ring on which there is an image, it is permissible to seal with it. R. Hanania b. Gamaliel says: [they] of my father's household would seal with a signet having images' (Tosefta, Abodah Zarah v:2).

Another seal impression was found only later, but also belonging to the same batch of documents. Since the two seal impressions tally with the number of the Greek letters sent by non-Jews, it is possible that they were actually attached to these letters. Such clay impressions are quite rare. The only other one known from the Bar-Kokhba period is from Murabba'at and was attached to a Jewish document (a deed of sale) bearing the date: 'Year Two of the Redemption of Israel in Jerusalem.'

The goat-skin with the batch of letters most probably belonged to the wife of Yehonathan son of Be'aya, who, when she fled with the others to the cave, took with her, in addition to the family belongings, part of the personal archive of Yehonathan – although it did not show him in a favourable light. Whatever we may think of Bar-Kokhba's harsh tone, it is quite clear that Yehonathan was not the most loyal of subordinates. Why he should carry with him the incriminating letters is anybody's guess; was it a memento of the illustrious but unfollowed leader? Or perhaps – to our modern way of thinking – an alibi for the confiscation of property? Whatever the case, Yehonathan and Masabala were not the only insubordinate commanders in Bar-Kokhba's army – at least not towards the end of the revolt. Nothing fails like failure!

In a cave twenty kilometres to the north of the Cave of Letters, in Wadi Murraba'at, another commander took refuge with his family: Yeshua ben Galgoula. He, too, carried with him some letters received from his subordinates and, above all, from Bar-Kokhba. These letters, as mentioned earlier, were partly bought from the Bedouins and partly found on the spot by Père R. de Vaux and his colleagues. They were published by a member of de Vaux's team, Father J. T. Milik.

The first of these letters to be discussed here is written to Yeshua ben Galgoula by the administrators of the village of Beth Mashkho, which came under the command of his 'camp'. In it his title is 'chief of the camp' (see page 135):

'From the administrators of Beth Mashko, from Yeshua and from Eleazar

to Yeshua ben Galgoula chief of the camp, peace. Let it be known:

to you that the cow which Yehoseph ben Ariston took from Ya'aqov

ben Yehudah, who dwells in Beth Mashko, belongs to him [i.e. to Ya'aqov] by purchase

were it not for the Gentiles [i.e. the Romans] who are near us, I would have gone up

and satisfied you concerning this, lest you will say that it is out of contempt

that I did not go up to you. Be you well and the whole House of Israel.

> Yeshua ben Eleazar has written it [i.e. dictated it]
> Eleazar ben Yehoseph has written it
> Ya'aqov ben Yehudah, for himself
> Sha'ul ben Eleazar, witness
> Yehoseph ben Yehoseph, witness
> Ya'aqov ben Yehoseph, testifies [scribe or notary?].'

There are some minor divisions of opinion among scholars concerning some details, but I believe that the meaning is quite clear. Yehoseph ben Ariston (a soldier of ben Galgoula?) took a cow from a resident of Beth Mashkho (wherever that was), which comes under the jurisdiction of the two administrators. They claim the cow on his behalf but cannot come to ben Galgoula because the Romans are in their vicinity. This last point shows that at that time Bar-Kokhba's units and the Roman units were stationed not far away from one another.

'Chief of the camp'

The main point, though, for us is that Yeshua ben Galgoula is 'chief of a camp' which explains better the letters addressed to him by Bar-Kokhba. Apart from that, we know little about him except for what we can gather from a Greek document, also found in Murabba'at. It is a contract of remarriage of ben Galgoula's sister, Salome. It is from this document, too, that we learn the vowels of his father's name; GLGLA(H), since in Hebrew only the consonants are given. The contract is dated Year Seven of Hadrian (also indicated by the consuls of that year), i.e. AD 124. We do not exactly know where his camp was, but the contract was drawn up in the district of Herodium near Bethlehem. This may explain the fact that Yeshua ben Galgoula later took refuge in the caves of Wadi Murabba'at, the canyon emanating from the vicinity of Herodium.

Amongst the two complete (although somewhat damaged)

'letters' written by Bar-Kokhba to ben Galgoula, the following is the more important:

> 'From Shimeon ben Kosiba to Yeshua
> ben Galgoula and to the men of the fort,
> peace. I take heaven to witness against me
> that unless you mobilise [destroy?] the Galileans who
>   are with you
> every man, I will put fetters
> on your feet as I did
> to ben Aphlul.'

A letter from Bar-Kokhba to ben Galgoula in which he threatens to put fetters on ben Galgoula's feet. The letter was found in Wadi Murabba'at

There is a sharp division amongst scholars about the word in line 4, which is damaged and illegible. It is quite clear though, that ben Galgoula was ordered to do something 'negative' to the Galileans. Bar-Kokhba is not sure that the order would be obeyed, so he resorts to an oath to strengthen his warning: ben Galgoula and his men shall be arrested; and lest ben Galgoula think this to be an idle threat, let him remember poor ben Aphlul, most probably a notorious case, of which unfortunately we know nothing.

This letter reminds me of the one in our cave in which Bar-Kokhba orders Yehonathan and Masabala not to give shelter to anyone from Tekoa. Isn't this case similar? The Galileans took refuge with ben Galgoula and he is ordered to punish them. The solution depends on the understanding of the word 'Galileans'. Some scholars interpret it as 'Christians', but this does not make sense for the term *Galilean*, without further qualification, was generally used to denote people from Galilee (including famous sages) and I believe it should be understood here in the same way. The only possibility, perhaps, in which the 'culprits' were not people from Galilee in the north of Israel, is to assume that a location called Galil – and unknown to us – existed in Judaea, and its people are referred to by Bar-Kokhba as *Galileans* in the same way as he calls the people of En-gedi *Engedites*.

'Send wheat'

The next letter of Bar-Kokhba is less menacing, and it concerns food supplies, although some words are unclear:

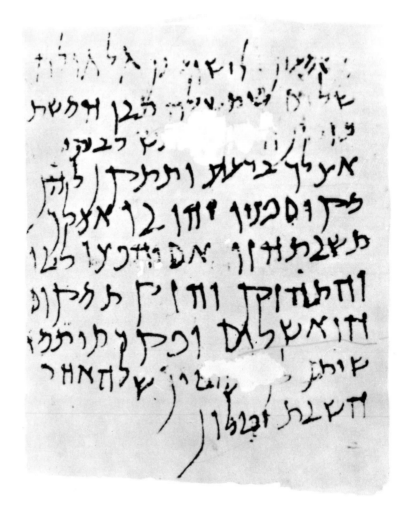

Another letter found in Wadi Murabba'at in which Bar-Kokhba requests wheat from ben Galgoula

'From Shimeon to Yeshua ben Galgoula,
peace! send cereals five
kors of wheat to. . . .

. . . .

Be strong and strengthen the place.
Be well.'

Then, a sort of *post scriptum*:

'I have ordered someone
to give you his wheat
after Sabbath they will take.'

A third letter is unfortunately very fragmentary, and even the names of the addressers and addressees are lost. More is the pity, since this letter refers to some military exploits or catastrophes; here are some intelligible phrases, a dirge whose pathos bridges the centuries in the mournful music of desolation and defeat:

'. . . till the end . . .
. . . they have no hope . . .
. . . my brothers in the south . . .
. . . of these were lost by the sword . . . .
. . . these my brothers. . .'

11 The second search

A year later

When the first attempt at deciphering the letters ended, some of our enthusiasm had to make way for more prosaic work such as the meticulous study of the clothing and the mats, and the registration, drawing and photography of the objects. Thus all of us sank back, more or less, into the grey daily routine, the common lot of the archaeologist who returns from the field with his 'loot'. Slowly but persistently, however, a thought kept nagging me that, with the high tension in the cave, we might have missed some pieces of cloth and mats, of which the importance became more evident as the study of those we had found progressed. It also became apparent that we needed a more accurate plan of the cave to facilitate the recording of the precise spots where the various finds were made. So I began to speculate about a possible second season of exploration and, at the beginning of 1961, the heads of the other teams came to a similar conclusion. The fact that we discovered so many objects in a cave which had already been examined in 1953 led Aharoni to the conclusion that he might want to re-examine the Cave of Horrors, explored by him in 1955. Avigad, too, thought he might return for a more systematic scrutiny of Nahal David, which he began to examine – in addition to his own sector A – only at the end of the previous season. These were quite logical assumptions. Bar-Adon, for no apparent reason, decided to have another try in the same cave he had just explored. I must say here that in retrospect I admire his decision because he came across a most remarkable find – although not from the period of Bar-Kokhba – which I shall describe later on.

From the experience of the previous season we knew that we could not embark on such an enterprise without the full co-operation and assistance of the Israel Defence Forces: not only because of the problems of supplies, camps and lines of communications, but because it was the army's generator which provided the light that helped us to discover some of the more outstanding finds we made, and the other heads of teams were eager to try again with electricity in their caves. The then Chief of Staff, Rav-Aluf Z. Tzur, agreed to co-operate, provided we could share some of the cost. So we embarked on a real fund-raising campaign in the form of lectures, dinners, and individual solicitations. The response was most encouraging. In a short meeting on 8 February with the Chief of Staff and some of his aides, it was agreed that the second expedition would set out on Sunday, 12 March 1961, thus allowing us over two weeks until Passover. It was also agreed that since by now we knew precisely which caves we wanted to tackle, our camps would be pitched right on top of the canyon banks, as close as possible to the individual caves. This was wise since it eliminated the need, as in the first season, of moving people daily by jeeps and command cars from their camps to the cliff edge above the caves. This time we could just step out of our bivouacs and descend directly.

A preliminary reconnaissance was sent out to the field (in which D. Ussishkin, my principal aide of the first season, represented me) to fix the exact siting of the camps and the ways of approach. As in the previous year, heavy rains began a few days before we started out, and we had to accede to the army's demand to postpone 'D-Day' to 14 March because the desert tracks were impassable.

In Beer-Sheva the four heads of teams met their respective team members. This time they included, in addition to Hebrew University students and volunteers from the *kibbutzim* and *moshavim*, a number of volunteer students from the United States, England, Sweden, France, Canada and Japan who happened to be in the country. The previous year's discoveries had kindled everybody's imagination and many wished to join us. Again, as in the previous year, the main task of organisation, administration and co-ordination fell to Joseph Aviram. So off we went to the desert, although the appellation 'desert' at that moment was not appropriate; because of the rains, which that winter had lasted longer than usual, the whole sandy waste looked green and was

Driving through the desert for the second season in military vehicles

studded with patches of beautiful coloured flowers. It was a sight that cheered our hearts and we needed that cheering too, since deep down we did not really dare to believe our luck would continue and give us another season with such outstanding finds.

After a tedious journey in military cars on the slippery roads, the little twinkling lights indicating the location of the camp beckoned to us in the distance. We arrived at nine o'clock at night, happy to know that members of an organised army unit were there to meet us. Having preceded us by a few days, they felt like veterans and welcomed us as if we were new immigrants.

Back to work

Next morning without much ado we descended to our cave. This time, however, the descent seemed much easier and the sense of danger on the ledge had almost gone. This was not only because of confidence gained in the previous year; it was mainly due to the wonderful work the army engineers had done in widening the paths and fixing a horizontal wooden ladder in the narrow crevice beyond the dangerous ledge. It made things so much easier that I wondered why we had not thought of that simple device the year before.

One disappointment was the discovery that Ginger was not with us this time, for reasons best known to the army. Instead, we were compensated by an engineering officer, known to his men as Johnny. He was quite a different character from Ginger, but it was due to him that all the technical arrangements were flawless. When we entered the cave, the new members of the team were disappointed to find it completely lit up. In a way I regretted this too, because it deprived them of the eerie feeling we had when we first entered the cave the year before in complete darkness, groping our way amongst the thousands of bats. One has to pay a price for progress . . . .

The team was allotted various tasks in small groups. The main force took over the first hall where the bronze objects were found the previous year. I made up my mind to excavate the whole area this time, to make quite sure that nothing would escape us. It was tedious work and nothing was found, but 'negative information is also information'! I admired the volunteers doing the difficult and dusty work in that hall, for the exciting discoveries were made in the other parts of the cave and shouts of excitement and joy used to reach them faintly back in the first hall while they had to stick – and they did stick – to their less rewarding jobs. In addition, small groups of twos and threes were assigned to re-examine the crevice of the letters, the niche of the skulls and clothing, the niche of the baskets and skeletons, and also to clean the second entrance to the cave.

At the beginning spirits were very high. Small bits of cloth and mats were found all over, and in the crevice where the letters were found – Bar-Kokhba's Post Office Box, as we called it – we discovered a second seal impression, similar to the one found in the previous year and described in Chapter 10. However, as work proceeded that first day and we reached the 'dangerous' early hours of the afternoon – at which time the little oxygen accumulated in the cave at night was already consumed – members of the team began to show first signs of sleepiness and lethargy, typical symptoms of lack of oxygen. At that moment Johnny, the engineer, came to inspect his technical arrangements and make sure they all worked. I accompanied him through the three halls. At one place we saw one of the elderly volunteers stretched out in a deep crevice. 'What are you doing here?' I asked. 'I am sleeping,' he said nonchalantly, so we hastened to shake and wake him. In the second hall we found a small team who told us they were convinced that nothing could ever be found where they were working – another symptom of the same lethargy. So, in order to revive their spirits, I moved them from the second hall to the third hall in the extreme depth of the cave, to a crevice which we had not inspected well enough previously, located on the left of that hall as you enter it. As we entered the third hall we were amazed at the ghost-like appearance of the workers there. 'Where do you expect to find the next discoveries?' asked Johnny with scepticism all over his face. Frankly I had no convincing answer. 'You never can tell,' I replied, 'but one just has to persist.' It was three o'clock in the afternoon when I accompanied Johnny back to the first hall and he departed.

Then, a few minutes later, Sefi (Yoseph Porath), a young volunteer from Kfar Vitkin who, as far as I knew, belonged to the group examining the crevice of the letters, rushed up to me panting and pale. 'I have found something important!' he cried. 'A basket filled with objects and nearby, all sorts of things.' Sefi was a restive fellow who was always on the go, inquisitive, curious about what was happening at other places. To him the grass elsewhere always looked greener. As soon as he saw the newly transferred group – just then moved by me to examine the crevice in the third hall – he went to 'visit' them and see what they were doing. 'And', he continued to tell me, 'just a few moments before I reached them I trod on a stone which wobbled suspiciously. So I removed it and under it I saw this crevice full of finds.'

I rushed back with him. In the cave this was not an easy thing. First one had to crawl through the narrow tunnel connecting the first and second halls, then jump like an acrobat over the huge and pointed boulders in the second hall. But somehow at that moment this seemed no hardship. We just ran. 'What is there in the basket?' I asked Sefi as we ran. Now he seemed more cautious: 'Esther' (a student of archaeology), he said, 'says that perhaps the basket contains scrolls.' Although I am an optimist by nature, a thought crossed my mind that perhaps this was a repetition of the

An incredible cache

143

hallucination that one of the soldiers had the year before when he mistook skulls for scrolls. Hope and doubt tumbled over each other in my mind in those moments. As we entered the third hall, left of the entrance, I saw Esther and some others, their faces alight with joy. Even from Sefi's description I did not expect the place to be so close to the entrance of the third hall which we had searched many times before. It was in fact the very place which Johnny and I had walked upon a little bit earlier while inspecting the cave. When I approached them I saw a crevice between big stones – from which Sefi had removed the wobbling stone – and below it there was still another crevice, about a metre deep. Inside I could see quite clearly a basket made of palm fronds, identical with the basket that had held the metal objects on our first expedition. This basket was indeed filled to the brim. 'Where are the scrolls?' I asked Esther. 'I am not sure there are any,' was her cautious reply, 'but here is an object that looks like one.' I stretched my arm into the basket, extricated the object, and found myself holding a strange box with coloured decorations; it was not a scroll. Then I lay flat on my belly and lowered my head into the crevice. Under the basket I could see a big water skin, similar to the one in which all the letters had been found, and beneath it, on a sloping stone, I could discern a number of other objects difficult to identify from above.

Waiting for the photographer I had to curb and control my own and my team's impulse to try and pull out the objects through the narrow opening created by the removal of the wobbling stone. I knew that we must on no account tackle the basket before removing at least two or three further stones of those deliberately placed to cover the cache, and this I did not want to do before photographs had been taken. Unfortunately Harris the photographer was at that moment with camp B, but since this year we had the luxury of field telephones inside the caves, we could communicate more easily with one another. I contacted the photographer, only to be informed that it would take him at least an hour and a half to reach us. By then it was nearly four o'clock and I realised that even if he were to reach us by 5.30 it would be too late to do anything that day. This was an operation that required time for meticulous recording of the location of every object, so reluctantly I decided to postpone it to the morrow. We invited all the workers from their assorted crevices and holes to come and admire the find *in situ* and it was fun listening to each of them speculating, according to their fantasy and imagination, about what they expected this cache to yield.

In high spirits we climbed back to our camp. What good fortune, and all in the first day! Yet none of us at that time imagined what a wonderful find this would turn out to be.

We did not sleep much that night. The morning brought not

left The basket of the cache as it was found when the wobbling stone had been removed. Note the narrow stones placed to hide the crevice
below The jewellery box – the first object to be removed from the basket

Waiting by the crevice for the photographer to arrive before removing the objects

only Harris, the expedition photographer, but also Micha Bar'am, the experienced explorer-reporter-photographer of the army weekly *Bamahaneh*. Somehow or other our news had filtered through to the other camps. We now planned our actions very carefully. I did not want too many people around, so most of the members of the team, to their understandable resentment, were sent off to the first hall to resume normal work. With me remained the students, my assistant Ussishkin, the photographers and the deputy commander of the camp, Captain Yefet, who was better known as Yoskeh (the same Yoskeh who several years later commanded the camp at Masada). We also took down with us wrappings and packing material, boxes, cotton-wool, etc. Subconsciously we must have shied away from showing over-optimism, so – not to invite disappointment – we did not take sufficient wrapping material with us, and were later compelled to keep sending people up to the camp for more. One final prosaic detail: we had to give the *locus* a number for the purpose of registration of the finds; the running serial number at that time was sixty-one, and so it will remain in the final scientific report. We arrayed ourselves around the crevice and everything was photographed *in situ*. Only then did we remove the additional stones covering the opening, and with much difficulty I pushed myself into the crevice. Ussishkin was on my right with the registration log, ready to record and describe every object handed out by me from the basket. Near him sat two students prepared to wrap anything, and above me, Yoskeh was holding an electric cable attached to a strong light which he shone into the crevice. The other students were standing all around ready to help. Complete silence descended, broken only by the whirring flight of bats.

The crevice after the stones hiding the cache had been removed

An exciting moment: starting to empty the basket

The first object to come out was the one suspected by Esther on the previous day to be a scroll. It was a wooden box, barrel-dome-shaped with a flat base, its exterior covered with very thin layers of deep yellow resinous material and further painted with yellow and red spots, arranged in regular rows, as well as two crossed bands, red and black, of the same resinous stuff. The bottom, that is to say the lid, was also covered by the same yellow stuff. It looked like a jewellery box. We could not open it there and then because we did not wish to force its catches which were attached to the sliding lid like old-fashioned pen cases, in which the lid fits into grooves on its two sides and into a slot at the far end of the box. The box turned out to be empty, but it was in itself a unique object.

The jewellery box and its sliding bottom

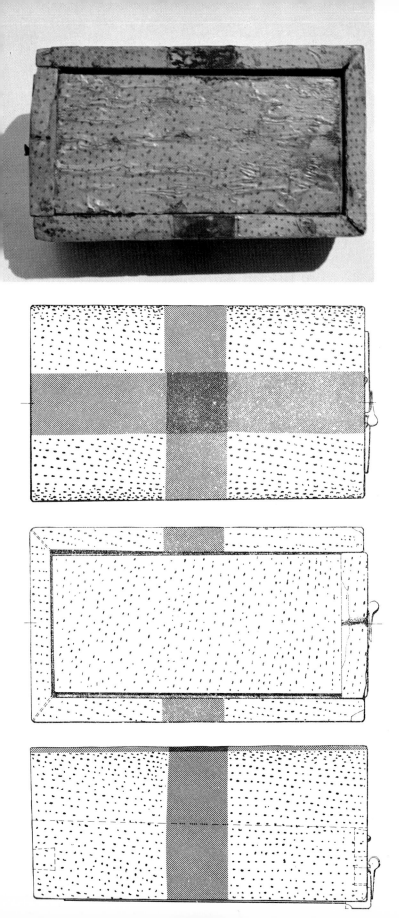

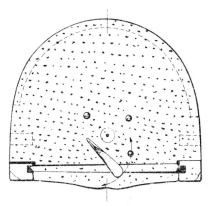

Bottom and side views of the
jewellery box with drawings of the box
showing some of its technical details

The four wooden bowls without any cleaning and (*right*) a side view of a bowl on which the marks of the lathe can be seen

Another view of one of the wooden bowls

The second objects to emerge were a set of four wooden bowls or plates, beautifully turned by lathe; they were perfectly clean, as if the last people to use them in the cave had scrubbed off the very last particles of food on them and scratched the bottom. Then came a simple curved iron sickle with a wooden handle, its inner sharp edge slightly saw-toothed. Obviously the fugitives still hoped to be able to use it some day. The jewellery box was a first indication that we might have found the cache of a woman and the next object to emerge strengthened this assumption; it was a pair of woman's leather sandals extremely well preserved. The two sandals did not seem to constitute one pair; one of them looked somewhat deformed, and indeed an orthopaedic specialist who saw them later, told me immediately that the wearer must

The iron sickle with a wooden handle

151

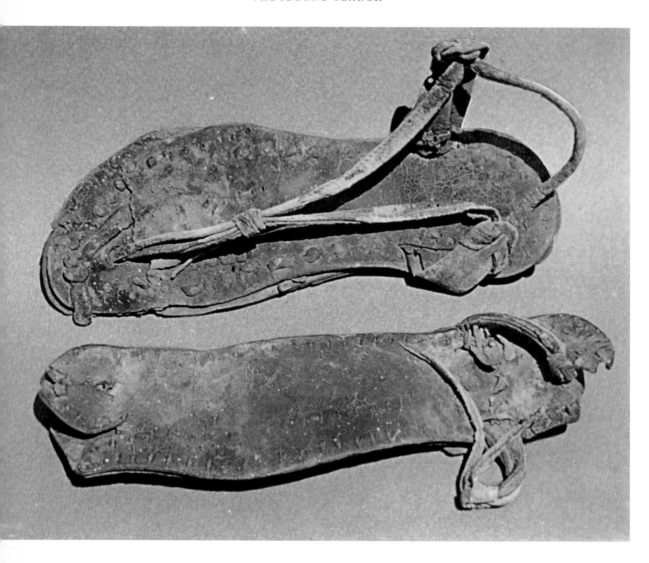

The pair of sandals found in the
basket; note that one sandal is
deformed. In style these sandals are
reminiscent of the more sophisticated
sandals of today
right A sandal found in Masada.
There is a striking similarity between
it and the sandals from the cave
although sixty years separate them

have limped and he diagnosed the cause of the limp. At that time we did not yet know that soon we would learn many more intimate details concerning that woman. Next came out three keys, two of them ring keys. As an archaeologist used mainly to pottery and sherds in an excavation, I found it thrilling just to stretch an arm into a basket and take out complete and intact objects, even of perishable material. Soon afterwards I took out a group of iron knives with wooden and bone handles; a set of cutlery which consisted of one heavy chopper and four other knives, one of them a folding pen-knife. Gazing at one most of us began to smile; its blade must have been sharpened and re-sharpened many times until its edge became concave, reminding everyone of us of the one and only sharp knife in every kitchen.

The knives found in the basket; note the chopper and the small, much-sharpened knife

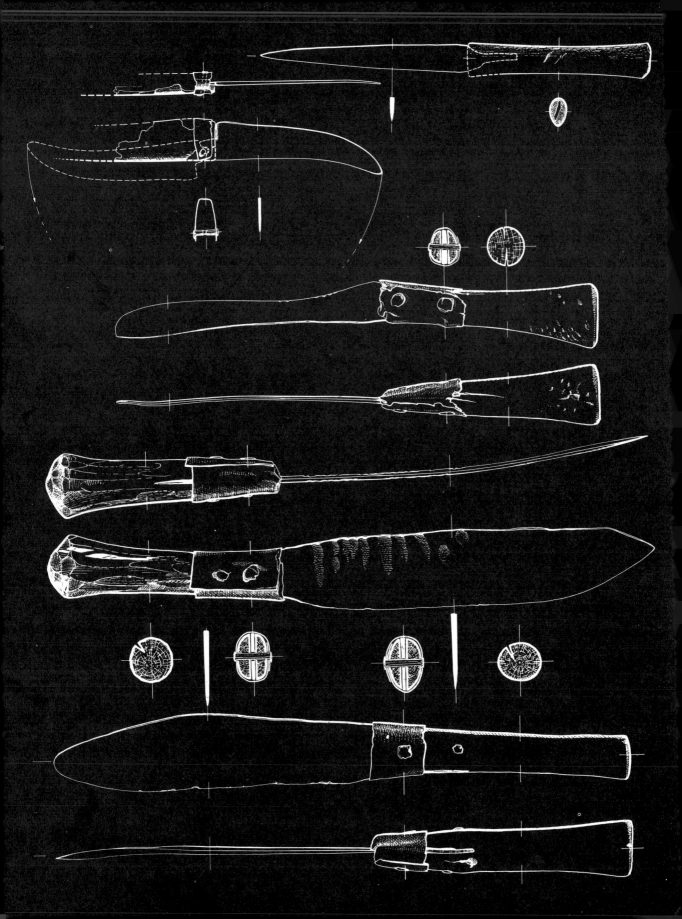

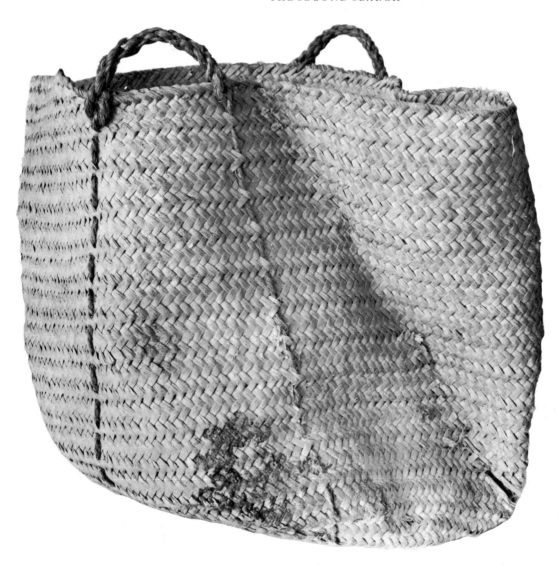

Once the basket had been emptied and its contents registered and photographed, we could remove it too and get a closer look at the crevice below it. On the slope to the right of the goatskin I could see a number of metal vessels, obviously fallen out of either the basket or the goatskin which looked torn and eaten up by worms. The first object brought up was a flat iron frying-pan on which heavy traces of soot were still visible. Nearby lay two bronze jugs, similar to those found in last year's basket. And if proof were still needed that this was a woman's cache, the next object provided it: a mirror, identical in shape and make with the one found last year in the crevice of the letters; as if both of them had been bought in the same supermarket in En-gedi. The metal disc was so shiny that we could easily see our dusty, sweating, radiant reflections in it.

The basket after its contents had been removed

opposite Drawings of the knives

155

above The mirror found in the crevice identical to the one found the year before near the Bar-Kokhba letters
opposite The iron frying-pan found in the crevice near the basket. It measured twenty-six centimetres in diameter and the hinging bars of its two horse-shoe shaped handles (extending twelve centimetres on either side) ran through sockets riveted to the pan proper. The sockets were forged from thin sheets of iron bent to the required shape

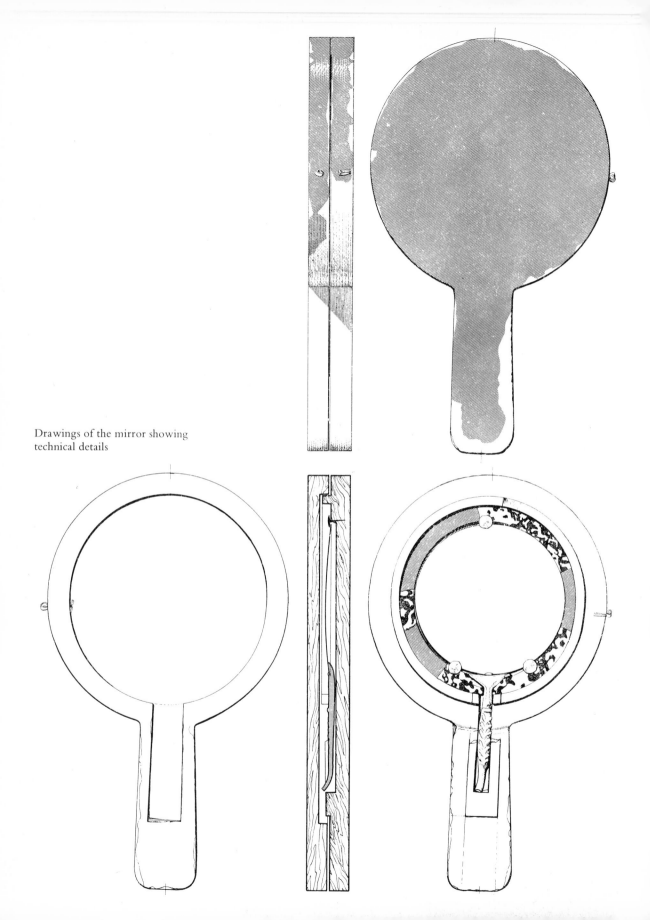

Drawings of the mirror showing
technical details

While pausing for the objects to be recorded, my mind busy with all sorts of wild thoughts concerning what we had already found, my eyes suddenly fastened on something else. At the bottom of the crevice lay a complete and rolled scroll of parchment with a string tied around it! I bent deep into the crevice, stretched my arm and brought it up. My colleagues who stood around say that my hand trembled and it may well be. It seemed that after all these efforts we had finally found a complete scroll. We could not, of course, open it there and then. I peeped into its inner parts through its end, yet could see no traces of writing. It crossed my mind this might be a blank scroll – just material prepared for writing – but I could not bring myself to say so aloud lest I dampen my colleagues' enthusiasm. Not far away lay a strange object, a reed or cane, some thirty centimetres long. 'A flute!' I exclaimed and took it out to show around. But in the light of the electric

The parchment scroll as it was found

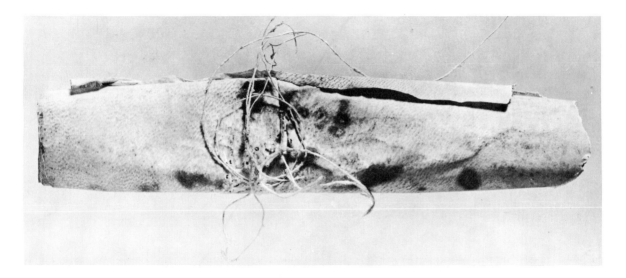

The 'flute' or reed case with the papyrus still inside

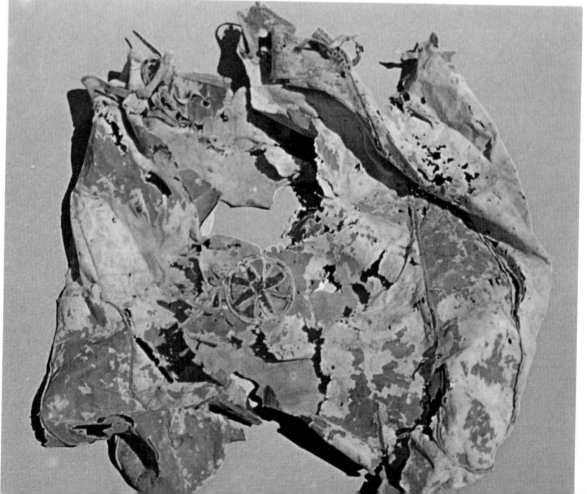

bulb it became clear that I was pleasantly deceived; there were no blowing holes in it and the reed was intact, encasing a papyrus document visible through its open end. Now we came to the centre of the crevice: that is to say to the heap of remains of the goatskin and fragments of clothing, sacks, and similar materials. The assembly of these, after the exhilarating moments of a few minutes earlier, was done, I admit, with lessened tension. But suddenly my hand gripped what looked like a small cigar, or cigarillo, five to six centimetres in length by one centimetre in diameter: an intact papyrus! It was rolled several times and seemed complete. A feverish search in the same spot ensued and five more such papyri came up. Some were rolled like the first, some were extremely well folded, and two were still tied by palm-frond cords. This group of papyri were all bunched together and it soon became apparent that they did not fall from the goatskin but had originally been in a small leather pouch or purse, which was found torn and moth-eaten near it. It is possible that even the reed cane had originally belonged in this pouch. Exactly the same type of purse is mentioned several times in the Talmud, for example: 'If a purse with a draw-string lose a string it is still susceptible to uncleanness, but if it is ripped open, it becomes unsusceptible' (Kelim XXVI:2). That is, a purse from which the draw-string has been removed is still usable, for it is still possible to tie it. If, however, it is opened flat, that is if the seams have been ripped open and the purse has been returned to the form of a flat sheet of leather, then it is considered unusable. From a similar find of the Roman period in Holland, we know that that type of purse was actually used to keep money in. Probably our purse served to keep in it the papyri which we found.

Packing of papyri requires special care, and so we had to take a break. Each papyrus was then wrapped individually in cotton-wool and put in a separate box tied by string, on which its number, its description, its state of preservation and its exact location were recorded.

opposite above A close-up of the 'flute'

The 'cigar', a small intact papyrus, as it was found

opposite below and left The leather purse or pouch as it was found. The purse was thirty-four centimetres square and was made of a long piece of red dyed leather, folded over in the middle. Round the top, holes were punched through which a draw-string was threaded. In one of the upper corners there was a sort of carrying handle, like a braided thong ending in a knot. The drawing of the reconstructed purse illustrates these details

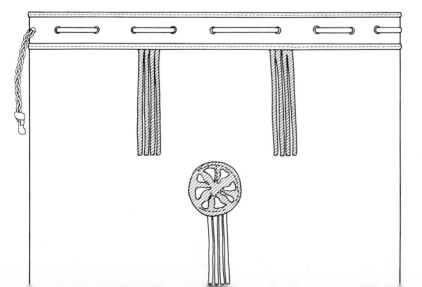

opposite Two of the moth-eaten goatskins after cleaning

A dramatic moment: gripping the goatskin bag. Note the ropes tying the end of the skin

Now at last, came the turn of the goatskin, and we could examine it more closely, although we already knew that it was badly torn and eaten by moths and worms. It was a rather large goatskin and one end of it, the original back of the animal, was well tied with rope made of palm fronds. (When we examined all its remains in Jerusalem later, we came to the conclusion that what we had were three bags, although on the spot they looked like one only.) I began to empty its contents. The veterans who were with us the previous year and had witnessed the emptying of the goatskin with the letters, started smiling when they saw my hand

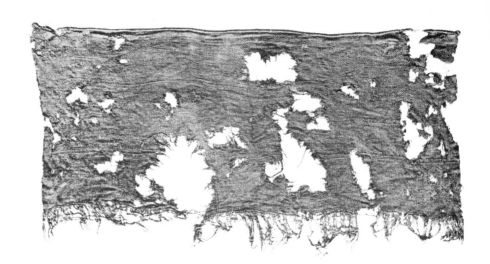

come up with big skeins of yarn, similar to those we found in the bag of letters, with one difference though; the former were of wool, while these were all flax. I rummaged at the bottom of the bag and found a great number of rags, pieces of tunics, sacks, ropes and yarn – everything, in fact, that a woman would need for mending her family's clothes. When I thought that I had emptied the bag completely, I raised it by its ends and put it carefully into a large box handed to me by Ussishkin. Before closing that box I again examined the torn inside of the goatskin just to be sure that I had not overlooked anything, and suddenly my hand came up against a package which at first felt like an additional bundle of rags, although it was carefully tied by palm-frond strings, length and crosswise. I lifted it, looked at it and could not believe my

opposite A linen sheet and detail of a sheet found with the goatskin bags

The balls or skeins of linen thread found in the goatskin

eyes: scores of papyrus rolls, stuffed together like a bunch of asparagus, confronted me from the open end of the bundle. Without even counting them I guessed there were about forty or so. My first reaction was 'Incredible!' – followed quickly by the spoken fear that it might be just stationery – blank papyri which the fugitives took with them to the cave for future use! Not one of those around me was willing to accept such a possibility. I, too, did not wish to believe it. But if this were not just writing material, then – to judge by the quantity at least – what we had come upon would be the greatest cache of written documents discovered up to that time in a single bundle anywhere in the Judaean Desert. What was in it? The answer had to await our return to Jerusalem when the bundle could be properly opened.

Due to our great excitement and the dramatic developments lunchtime went by unnoticed. We were feverishly busy for nearly six hours. Then, when everything was ready, all of us proceeded in line towards the entrance of the cave, each carrying a box or two, yet for once not running, just walking very carefully and slowly, sometimes crawling on our bellies with the precious boxes held above our heads. And here we faced an immediate problem: how were we to take these treasures out of the cave, down the ladder and up the dangerous path to our camp? As a rule, every expedition has one member who is a special 'character', and if there was one amongst us this time who deserved that particular

A side view of the big archive, showing the scores of neatly packed documents

opposite The big archive of papyri as found. Note the meticulous wrapping and packing: the leather purse is inside

definition, it was undoubtedly Mussa, who now came to our rescue. Mussa was a veteran petty officer in the Israeli navy, with the appropriate yardage of moustache. He was sent to us as an expert on rope ladders and climbing – which was exactly what this kind of operation required. If you can visualise a fish out of water put on dry land, you should be able to imagine Mussa's feelings at the beginning of the expedition. He worked extremely hard and well, but kept grumbling constantly about crazy archaeologists, and particularly about the 'dryness' of the desert, by which he meant the lack of liquor. However, in a very short while the archaeological 'bug' infected him badly, and his wonderful sense of humour and ability were of invaluable assistance to us. (A few years later, Mussa became my main technical assistant and safety

Mussa, the sailor, preparing a rope ladder

officer at Masada and Hazor.) The news of the extraordinary discovery of our cache had reached Mussa's ears, and soon enough he was there. So I entrusted him with the delicate job of transferring the boxes from the cave to the camp. While he was lowering the boxes on the rope ladder it seemed to me for a moment that he was not treating them with enough respect.

'Be careful,' I said to Mussa, 'This is a very important find. Take it easy.'

'Don't worry,' he replied. 'I treat it as if it were a case of whisky bottles, and what can be more precious than that?' But in his heart and behind the gruff exterior, as all of us knew well, he too realised that some things were much more precious than whisky, and what he held in his hand was one of them.

Mussa begins the descent with boxes of 'treasures'

Carrying the documents to the helicopter with Carmella and Art Buchwald for their transportation back to Jerusalem

In the evening all of us returned to the camp, very tired but very happy. The students who were in the camp had meanwhile opened some of the boxes and displayed their contents for the benefit of those members of the team who were busy elsewhere during the day. Except for the scroll, the reed cane, the papyri and the big bundle, which were packed ready for Jerusalem, everything was put on the tables in the common tent. Only as we gazed at all these objects before us did we realise, for the first time, how rich had been our crop in that cache. The most impressed were the new members of the team who had not shared our excitement the year before. Only the previous evening before we went to sleep, we showed them slides of the finds of the previous season to pep them up a bit. Indeed, it was very difficult now to refrain from commenting on the unusual similarity between the two caches. Both of them contained lots of feminine objects, skeins of yarn, and mirror sets, and both had a bundle of documents. The one yielded the letters of Bar-Kokhba, and the other? This we did not yet know.

A precious cargo

The weekend found all the members of the expedition in very high spirits. Most of us walked for several hours through the canyons to En-gedi to wash properly in its wonderful springs and peel off several layers of dust which had caked on our bodies that week. Our water in the camp was very limited indeed – one water flask per person per day for all functions. On Friday I had been informed through the Southern Command of the army that I might expect the visit of the well-known columnist Art Buchwald, who would come by hired helicopter on the morrow. I was very happy to learn this piece of news for two reasons: firstly because according to the message, my wife, Carmella, would accompany him and secondly because it occurred to me that this might be the best way to send the precious documents to Jerusalem. Sitting in a camp in the desert, searching for traces of Bar-Kokhba, one has a feeling of being almost on another planet, and then suddenly the landing of a tiny helicopter near the Roman camp transports one back to civilisation over thousands of miles and millennia.

We watched the helicopter depart amidst clouds of dust and were relieved to know that in a short while the documents would be safe in Jerusalem. Mussa, like a true sailor who has no faith in either the air force or the army, and feels secure only in a boat rocking on the high seas, looked at the tiny bubble in the air and said: 'Don't you think it is risky to send the papyri by helicopter to Jerusalem?' Then he caught himself and added with a wink: 'Well, if it is safe for Carmella, then I assume it is safe for the papyri too. . . .'

12 'The Redemption of Israel'

'The Third Year of Shimeon ben Kosiba President of Israel'

One of the achievements of the Signal Corps of the Israel Defence Forces for our expedition was the installation of wireless telephones in each of the caves, which enabled us to dial directly to any number we wished on the outside. So, a few days after our arrival in camp, I telephoned my home in Jerusalem and talked to Carmella. She told me that Bieberkraut had succeeded in opening some of the 'cigars', and according to him they were beautifully preserved and written. She also told me that she expected to visit us in the field at the end of the week. It seemed that Allan Bronfman, one of the most devoted governors of the Hebrew University (who had helped us in the past very generously with the publication of the results of the excavations at Hazor), was in the country and wanted to visit us. So Carmella hitched a ride with him in his hired helicopter. Since Bieberkraut, with all his abilities in opening scrolls, cannot read Hebrew script, I asked Carmella to go to him and try and read some of the documents before she came to visit us, or at least to see in what script they were written.

When the helicopter arrived, Bronfman went to the big tent to see our finds up to date, which had been laid out for him on a table. Carmella and I went into a small tent and there she gave me several sheets of paper which were her first attempt in deciphering the writing. She was ecstatic about the script, more beautiful and better preserved – she said – than the letters of Bar-Kokhba. She had indeed managed to read the beginning of one of the documents: 'On the twenty-eighth of Marheshvan, the third year of Shimeon ben Kosiba, President of Israel.' With due respect to her achievement, I felt quite certain that the script on that document must indeed be well preserved and relatively legible.

After letting my first enthusiasm subside, Carmella then gave me a bitter pill to swallow: the 'complete scroll' which we found was empty! No traces of script on it! It must have been writing material as I feared. This was a blow indeed, and I did not tell it to my colleagues at the time. Now the lingering suspicion that perhaps even the big bundle of papyri was nothing but stationery got slightly stronger. The rest of the days in the field were very tantalising for me. I submitted the empty 'scroll' to further examination by the criminal department of the Israel Police, to see if it had some invisible traces of script, only to learn that after having photographed it in infra-red and ultra-violet processes and tested it by various means, the police were sure that it had not been used.

On Tuesday, 28 March, we left the caves and camps and returned to Jerusalem. After a ·brief rest and thorough scrubbing and cleansing, I hurried in the afternoon to Bieberkraut to see for myself the five documents already opened. Old Bieberkraut and his wife welcomed me with shining eyes. They could not, and did not, wish to hide their happiness that again, as with the Dead Sea Scrolls and the Bar-Kokhba letters, it was their privilege to be the first to open the Hebrew documents written a couple of thousand years ago. Indeed, from the time that they received the documents from Carmella to this moment, they had worked day and night: he, to unroll the documents, and she, to photograph them by both infra-red and regular films. They now presented to me the five opened and photographed documents, framed between two thin sheets of glass. Although I was prepared to expect beautiful documents, I was really startled when I saw the clarity of the script on these. Unlike the hastily, cursively written letters, these were written by an expert official scribe. The script was similar to the printed Hebrew of today. This was the first time we had seen that script on deeds from the time of Bar-Kokhba; up till then we knew it only from fragments of the Bible. The lines were quite straight despite the fact that the scribe did not make use of horizontal ruling. At the end of some of the lines, where the remaining space was insufficient for a whole word, the scribe marked an X to prevent anyone from forging or adding anything to this official deed. At the bottom there were several lines of visible signatures. Three of the documents, written in Hebrew, were by the hand of the same official scribe. The other two were written in Aramaic by a less expert hand. I took the photographs with me and rushed back home to start reading them. I was engulfed by a strange feeling; the same that had pervaded me when I first read the Bar-Kokhba letters: the feeling of being physically in touch with people who had lived a thousand years ago.

The fact that the 'scroll' was empty led me immediately to investigate the document in the cane case. Was this too empty? I consulted Bieberkraut who expressed some doubts about the possibility of extricating the papyrus intact from the cane. I decided therefore to ask for the assistance of my friend Professor Beller, the noted brain surgeon at the Hadassah Medical Centre in Jerusalem. 'Can you operate on this "patient"?' I asked. He looked at it carefully and said he would try. It was an unusual sight to see Aviram, Bieberkraut, Harris the photographer and myself entering Dr Beller's clinic with its terrifying instruments. Automatically Beller started to disinfect his scalpel when he caught himself and smiled. Very skilfully, by 'nibbling' off bits at one end, he exposed the edge of the document and extracted it with forceps. His hands seemed to be shaking, and when I commented on this, jokingly, he said: 'I really do not remember ever being so nervous at an operation.' The operation was successful, though the 'patient'

The documents revealed

A brainwave

The 'flute' or reed case (*top right*) and the document found inside it

Dr Beller 'operating' on the 'flute' in his clinic

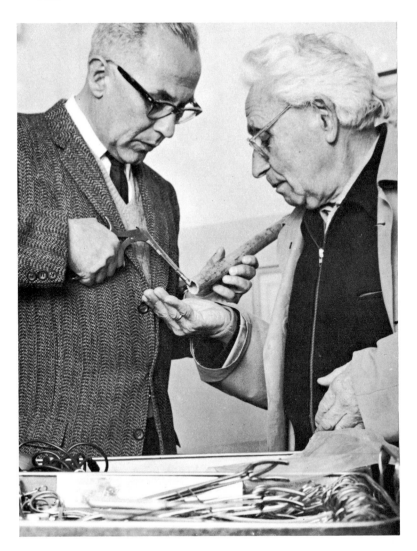

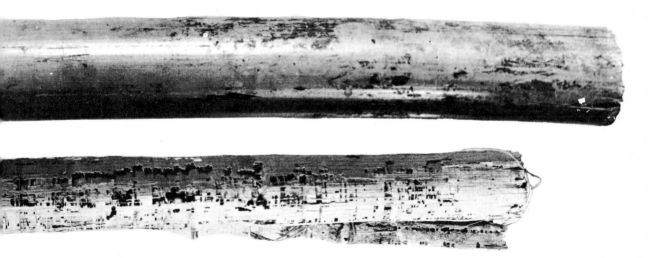

almost died, and not through the surgeon's fault. The extricated document was badly damaged by moths and worms, but enough remained to show that it, too, belonged to the Bar-Kokhba period.

The documents in the leather purse deal with various land transactions, mainly between the official administrators of Bar-Kokhba in En-gedi and private citizens. The lands of En-gedi (or certain parts of them) – which during the Roman occupation were 'crown lands' (as learnt from other documents to be discussed later) – are now leased on Bar-Kokhba's behalf, by 'the administrator of Bar-Kosiba, President of Israel, in En-gedi'. It is amazing how quickly the administrative set-up began to operate. Some of the documents bear the date of 'Year One' of Bar-Kokhba. Close examination of the contents of these documents will enlighten us on many facets of daily life as well as on the manner and style of writing documents in Mishnaic times. Let us therefore begin with a group of three Hebrew deeds, all of about the same date, all written by the same scribe and all referring to the same people. The deeds are of the 'simple' type, i.e. written on one side of the sheet only, with the signatures of the witnesses at the bottom, as against the 'tied' deeds (of a permanent nature) which will be discussed later on. As we shall see, the first deed concerns four people who had leased land nationalised under Bar-Kokhba, and who now wished to set down the perimeters of each one's portion. They negotiated with Yehonathan as the administrator for 'Shimeon ben Kosiba, President of Israel, at En-gedi', and the deed fixes the annual rent that each shall pay to the State. In the second deed, Eleazar, one of the four named in the first deed, sublets part of his leased land to one of the other partners, Eliezer. A surprising discovery is that this deed is dated only a few days after the first; which leads to a suspicion that perhaps a man was allowed to lease directly only a certain amount of 'crown lands', and this second deed was a device to circumvent the law if a man wanted to farm more land

Administrator of
Bar-Kokhba in En-gedi

than his legal entitlement. And if it were a trick, perhaps it failed: for one of Bar Kokhba's letters ordered the arrest of Eleazar and the confiscation of his lands.

The lease transaction

The first deed is written on a long sheet of papyrus (twenty-seven centimetres), and consists of twenty-six lines with an average of eight words to a line, two hundred words in all. The document begins in this way: 'On the twenty-eighth of Marheshvan, the third year of Shimeon bar Kosiba, President of Israel; at En-gedi. Of their own free will, on this day, do Eleazar son of Eleazar son of Hitta and Eliezer son of Shmuel, both of En-gedi, and Tehina son of Shimeon and Alma son of Yehudah, both of Luhith in the coastal district of 'Agaltain, now residents of En-gedi, wish to divide up amongst themselves the places that they have leased from Yehonathan son of Mhnym the administrator of Shimeon ben Kosiba, President of Israel, at En-gedi.'

Two of the parties mentioned are permanent residents of En-gedi, where the deed was drawn up, but the other two originate from Luhith. In subsequent documents we encounter other residents of the 'coastal district of 'Agaltain' – in the Provincia Arabia at the southern end of the Dead Sea – several years before Bar-Kokhba, who later on moved to En-gedi. It is clear that when the Bar-Kokhba Revolt began, Jews from areas outside the Jewish state were obliged to flee to areas within the Bar-Kokhba domain. This document enables us to identify the locality of Luhith, mentioned in Isaiah 15:5 in the description of the invasion of Moab: 'My heart cries out for Moab; his fugitives flee to Zoar, to Eglath-she-lishiyah. For at the ascent of Luhith they go up weeping. . . .'

And lastly, the administrator, Yehonathan son of Mhnym, is the addressor of one of the letters from Murabba'at. Thus we know that he was the administrator of En-gedi in the 'third year'.

After precise specification of the plots, the document states which lands have been allocated to the first two lessees, who apparently decided to stick together, and which to the other two separately. It then proceeds to enumerate the newly divided terms of payment: 'All is done and agreed on condition that the above four people will pay the dues of the lease of these places which they leased from Yehonathan son of Mhnym, as follows: Eleazar son of Eleazar Hitta and Eliezer son of Shmuel both will pay half of the money [the previously agreed amount] less sixteen *dinars*, which are four *Sela'im* only; while Tehina son of Shimeon and Alma son of Yehudah will pay half of the above money plus sixteen *dinars*, which are four *Sela'im*.' In these documents, as in those from Murabba'at and indeed in the Mishna, the money is referred to both in its newly given Hebrew name, *sela*, and in its 'foreign currency' value. The fact that the *sela* is equal to four silver *dinars* means that the famous Bar-Kokhba *tetradrachma* (= four *dinars*) was called *sela*.

The signatures of the four lessees are instructive. The first signed very crudely, in his own hand: 'Eleazar son of Eleazar, in person'. The other three must have been illiterate and could not even sign their names, so the formula of their signatures is as follows: 'Tehina son of Shimeon in person, written by Siton son of Shimeon at his dictation'. From this and from other documents, it can be inferred that the expression 'in person' did not indicate that the signature was in the signatory's own hand, but merely that he was one of the parties to the deed, as distinct from the witnesses who added the word 'witness' beside their name. The signatures of the witnesses followed immediately those of the parties, for example: 'Yehudah son of Yehoseph, witness'.

The first Hebrew deed as found and the top lines of this deed. It begins 'On the twenty-eighth of Marheshvan the third year of Shimeon bar Kosiba, President of Israel; at En-gedi.' It deals with the division of a lease. Note the X marks at the end of lines

A suspicious sequence

The second document – one of the 'cigars' – is also written on a narrow papyrus (five and a half by twenty-three centimetres) by the same scribe; thirty lines with an average of four words per line. It begins: 'On the second of Kislev, in the third year of Shimeon ben Kosiba, Prince of Israel; at En-gedi.' The former division had hardly come into effect, when already Eleazar leases to his partner Eliezer son of Shmuel, part of the land jointly leased by them: 'Eleazar son of Eleazar son of Hitta from En-gedi, said to Eliezer son of Shmuel of there: I today hereby acknowledge to you that I have leased to you our grove . . . my share with you of the land that we have leased, you and I, from Yehonathan son of Mhnym, the administrator of Shimeon ben Kosiba, President of Israel.' The deed then defines exactly the boundaries of the plot, and the legal rights of the lessee: 'You shall have the right to sow and collect for yourself all the fruits and crops which the place will yield.' Then comes a clause about the duration of the lease, which is interesting in so far as it does not specify it in terms of date, but 'until the termination of the season of the groves in En-gedi'. Eleazar receives for the lease twelve silver *zuzim* (i.e. *dinars*) which are 'three *Sela'im*'. The deed ends with a declaration of indemnity of the lessee from any claim connected with the area leased. It is signed by 'Eleazar son of Eleazar in person' followed by three witnesses. One of the witnesses is Masabala son of Shimeon.

opposite A detail of the other Hebrew deed showing the fine handwriting and the X marks. The word En-gedi (עין גדי) can be clearly read
below The top lines of the same deed which begin 'On the second of Kislev, in the third year of Shimeon ben Kosiba, President of Israel; at En-gedi'

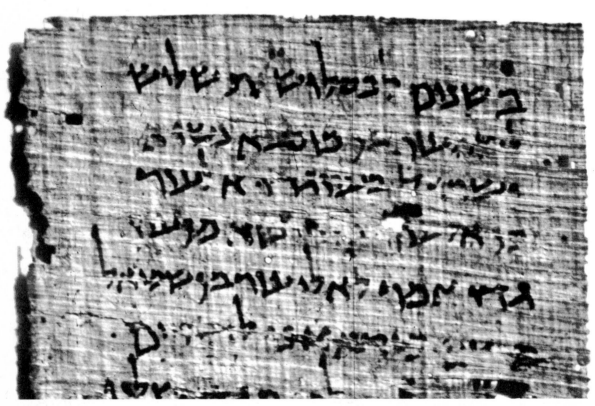

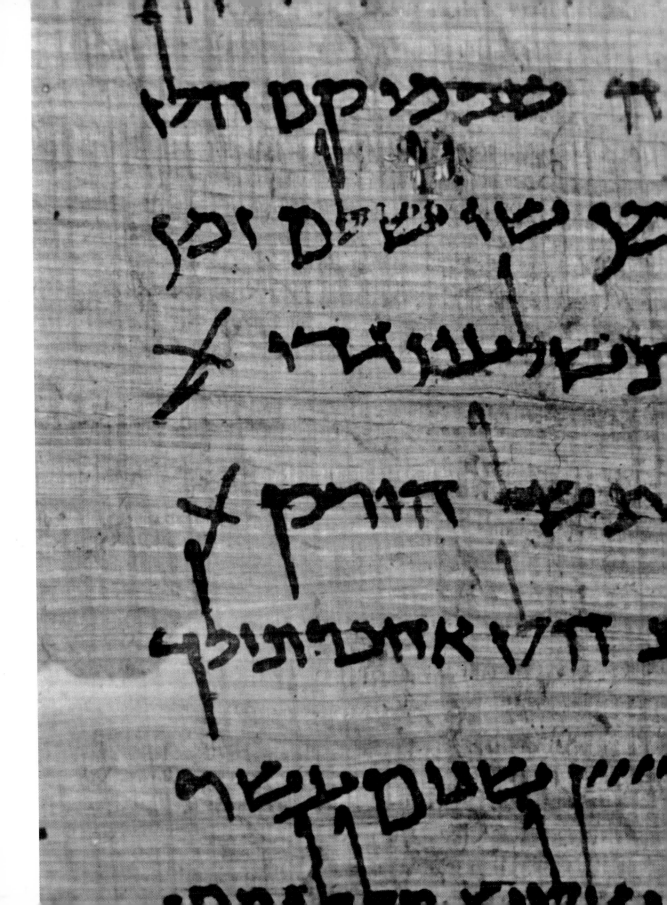

A problem of decipherment

The third document written by the same scribe and dated as the former, is very interesting indeed. It consists of a rectangular piece of papyrus (fifteen by seventeen centimetres) bearing eleven long lines. Here, both partners (Eleazar and Eliezer) together lease out to a third person, Ya'akov son of Shimeon some of the plots in their share of the original distribution of the land. This Ya'akov, acknowledges the lease and also signs 'in person'. This bond is particularly rich in Mishnaic terms and contains a great deal of information about the various kinds of fruits growing in En-gedi. The following episode is a good example for both. I had some difficulty in deciphering one line which defines the types of dates mentioned in the deed. I managed to read as follows: 'The fine [or: good] date . . . in the village'. The missing word after the 'fine date', relatively well preserved, looked to me like 'and the court' (חצר – HSR). When I consulted Professor Saul Lieberman, the greatest living Talmudist, about some Mishnaic problems in the documents, he immediately said to me (without even looking at the photograph): 'Can you read perhaps חצד (HSD) instead of HSR?' (The letters R [ר] and D [ד] in Hebrew are very similar.) He was right, I could. The reason for his suggestion was the fact that in the Mishna, Abodah Zarah (Paganism) 1:5, it is written: 'These things it is forbidden to sell to the gentiles . . . R. Meir says: Also "fine date", or Hasad or Nicolaus dates.' The sale of these expensive kinds of dates to gentiles was forbidden because the pagans used them to produce incense and as idolatrous oblations. The *Halakha* (the religious ruling) attributed to Rabbi Meir – which uses exactly the same terminology as our deed – was presumably intended for En-gedi and the surrounding district, where date-palms of this sort grew. These dates were so famous that Pliny the Elder, when describing the dates of Judaea in his *Historia Naturalis*, singles out the 'fine dates' and particularly the 'Nicolaus'.

The same document also defines the period of the lease in agricultural terms: 'until the terminations of the season of the crops of En-gedi: of the vegetables and of the trees'.

The money paid for this transaction was rather considerable – compared with sums mentioned in the other documents – one hundred and sixty silver *dinars*, 'which are forty *Sela'im*'.

'The First Year of the Redemption of Israel'

The other two documents, although badly preserved, are of much interest too. They are written in Aramaic and are the earliest documents of the Bar-Kokhba period in our possession. One is dated: 'On the first day of 'Iyyar [the second month in the regnal year] in the first year of the redemption of Israel by Shimeon ben Kosiba, President of Israel.' In this very crudely written document, the two administrators of En-gedi (Yehonathan son of Mhnym of the third year is not amongst them this time), lease out a plot of land to Eliezer son of Shmuel for six hundred and fifty *dinars* a year! This large amount covers the lease of everything in the plot, including the irrigation rights: '. . . and its water periods as proper and fit for them'. The irrigation arrangements at En-gedi – using the well-known spring waters especially channelled down the slopes – were very carefully worked out, the water being allocated to every plot according to specific quotas. The contract is in effect from the date at the top of the document ('from this day') and the lessee undertakes to pay the lease money in three annual, dated instalments of 300, 250 and 100 *zuzim* (*dinars*); since the lease was for four years, it is obvious that when Eliezer fled to the cave the deed was still in force.

The other document is of a few months later. It is short and in it the administrator acknowledges the receipt from Eliezer son of Shmuel of a certain amount of money, most probably 'on account', since it does not tally with the payments specified above.

The document in the reed case was badly preserved, but enough remains to read the name of Eliezer ben Shmuel. It may therefore safely be assumed that he was the owner of the leather purse with these documents, and it is on his behalf that Masabala signs.

The reed case

It is interesting that the earlier documents are written in Aramaic while the later ones are in Hebrew. Possibly the change was made by a special decree of Bar-Kokhba who wanted to restore Hebrew as the official language of the state.

Hebrew, the official language

Although the Hebrew documents were all written officially by formal scribes, the spelling includes some colloquialisms. For example the Hebrew definite accusative **את** (= the) is always written without the initial letter, and the second letter (**ת**) is joined to the noun, such as **תמקומות** instead of **את המקומות**. The equivalent in English would be 'thplaces' instead of 'the places'. The same phenomenon exists in the letters of Bar-Kokhba, and was thought to be a vulgarism. Now we realise that this usage was common also in official documents, and it is a phonetical way of writing, since the article was pronounced that way. Very similar is the enunciation in Hebrew used by children today.

A couple of weeks before we departed for the desert the second time, the official publication of the documents from Murabba'at came out. In Chapter 10 we have already discussed the letters of Bar-Kokhba which were among them. It is appropriate to con-clude the present review with one of the Murabba'at deeds, because of its similarity to those of En-gedi. This document, number twenty-four in the Murabba'at volume, is a wide papyrus, which comprises several columns containing an extract of lease deeds. It belongs to the type known in Greek as *diastroma*, and similar ones were also found in Egypt (but not of the Bar-Kokhba period). In each column there is the date, the name of lessors and lessees, the duration of the lease, and its terms. In this case most of the lands were grain fields, and payment was not in money but in kind: a certain amount was to be paid annually to the 'treasury'.

The lease documents from Murabba'at

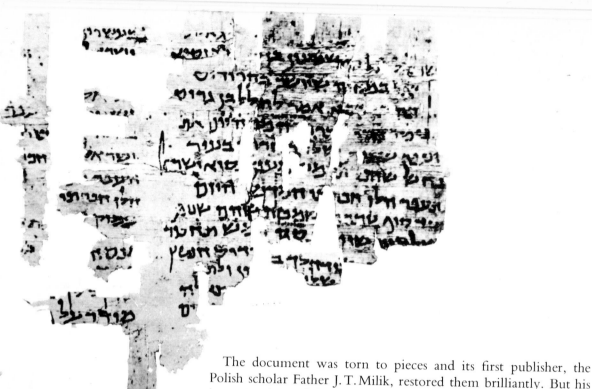

The lease document from Murabba'at. The top lines read 'On the twentieth of Shevat, Year Two of the redemption of Israel by Shimeon ben Kosiba, President of Israel. In the camp which is at Herodium'

The document was torn to pieces and its first publisher, the Polish scholar Father J. T. Milik, restored them brilliantly. But his interpretation of the beginning of the document did not make sense to me: 'On the twentieth of Shevat, Year Two of the liberation of Israel; By the authority of Shimeon ben Kosiba, President of Israel in campaign, who resides in Herodium. Yehudah son of Rabbah has said to Hillel son of Garis.' So, according to Milik, the document was issued by Bar-Kokhba whose headquarters were in Herodium. Accordingly Milik restored even the signature at the end of the document to read 'Shimeon ben Kosiba, by his order'. A few days before departing for the Cave of Letters, I wrote a short article titled 'Was Bar-Kokhba's headquarters in Herodium?' In it I suggested that the beginning of that document should read as follows: 'On the twentieth of Shevat, Year Two of the liberation [or: redemption] of Israel by [!] Shimeon ben Kosiba, President of Israel. In the camp which is at Herodium, Yehudah son of Rabbah said to Hillel son of Garis.' It seemed clear that the words interpreted as 'by the authority' actually meant 'by', 'through', referring to the liberation of Israel, and were part of the date formula. I also suggested that the words 'in the camp which is at Herodium' indicate the place where the deed was issued, and not where Bar-Kokhba resided. Little did I know then that a few weeks later we would discover the deeds from 'En-gedi clearly proving this interpretation. In our case En-gedi was the place of issue, instead of Herodium. Thus the document from Murabba'at contains a list of lands leased by Hillel son of Garis to various persons.

It is worth-while to quote some passages from these deeds for the additional light they shed on the elaborate system of Bar-Kokhba's administration. After the beginning, the texts go on: 'I, of my free will, have leased from you today the land ... which you leased from Shimeon ben Kosiba, Prince of Israel. This land I have leased from you as from today until the end of the eve of the *Shemittah* [remission year], which are five complete years, that is harvest-fiscal years.' The document then defines the payment which is to be weighed 'at Herodium [in] good and pure wheat: three *kors* and one *letek*'. There is no need to assume that Hillel son of Garis was an administrator; he could have been, like some of the people of En-gedi, a landowner who leased lands from Bar-Kokhba and then sub-leased them. However, the two important points in these documents are the fact that in Year Two there was a military camp, i.e. a garrison of Bar-Kokhba at Herodium, and the reference to the year of remission. Milik showed great ingenuity in his effort to make use of the dates in order to fix the absolute date of Year One, i.e. the beginning of the revolt.

The following are the known facts: first, the document was written in the month of Shevat, Year Two; second, the contract was to last to the end of the eve of the sabbatical (remission) year, i.e. five more complete years. Therefore, Year Two of the Bar-Kokhba era coincided with Year Two of the seven-year cycle of the remission years. If only we could count from any year of remission of which the absolute date is known, then we could also establish the date of Year Two, etc. Milik took as a starting point the Rabbinical tradition recorded in the Talmud, that the Temple was destroyed by Titus during *mosaei Shevi'ith*, which is interpreted by some as meaning 'the year after the sabbatical (or remission) year'. And since the Temple was destroyed in the summer of AD 70, the sabbatical year (preceding it) must have been from Tishri of 68 to Tishri of 69. (The sabbatical years were reckoned according to the Mishna from Tishri to Tishri; and the regnal years from Nisan to Nisan.) Counting from there, Milik arrived at the conclusion that year 130–1 was a sabbatical year, and thus the first year of Bar-Kokhba was from Tishri 131 to Tishri 132. This contradicted the accepted reckoning of the Bar-Kokhba years, which most scholars believed to have begun at AD 132–3. Thus Milik's conclusion could have been an important discovery, were it not for the fact that he regrettably counted incorrectly, as noticed by several scholars: if 68–9 was a year of remission then 131–2, and *not* 130–1, would have been another. The arithmetic is simple. Thus, *if* the allusion in the Rabbinical sources is correct, and *if* the interpretation of *mosaei Shevi'ith* is indeed the year after the sabbatical year, and not as some commentators think the sabbatical year itself, then according to the Murabba'at document Bar-Kokhba's first year was 132–3. Indeed, some *ifs*, but this date is confirmed by other sources mentioned in the first chapter, and also corroborated by the fact that the latest Roman coins re-struck by Kokhba are of the year 131–2.

Dating Year One of
Bar-Kokhba

13 Herodium, Qumran, Masada and Bethar

Herodium

Since Herodium (or Herodion in its Greek form) plays an important part in the Bar-Kokhba documents from Murabba'at, it is worth-while saying a few words about this site.

Herodium is the name of a fort which Herod the Great built at a place about seven miles south of Jerusalem and a couple of miles south-east of Bethlehem. It is situated on the border between the Judaean Desert proper and the fringe of the cultivated land. It lies about twenty-three miles north-west of En-gedi and in fact the old track from Jerusalem to En-gedi cuts through it. In this fort Herod also built his own tomb and there, according to Josephus, he was buried – hence its name. The ancient name of the site is preserved somewhat corrupted with the Arabs, as Jebel Fureides (i.e. 'Hill of Little Paradise'). The site was an important administrative centre of a sub-district of Judaea even before Bar-Kokhba. Bitter fighting took place there in the First Revolt. The site of the semi-artificial mound in which the palace was built looks like a woman's breast, to use Josephus's simile, and is even today a landmark which can be seen from a distance. In recent years the site was excavated by the Franciscan Father V. Corbo, and still more recently by the Department of Antiquities of Israel under the supervision of Mr G. Foerster. The excavations revealed the plan of this unusual palace: a circle, with three semi-circular towers and one round tower, which may have been the monarch's tomb. Inside were found many living quarters with a big bath, Roman style, with hot, tepid and cold rooms. Under the structure were found huge cisterns and many labyrinths of tunnels and corridors.

below The cone-shaped mound of Herodium seen from a distance
below right A plan of Herod's palace at Herodium; note the circular overall design

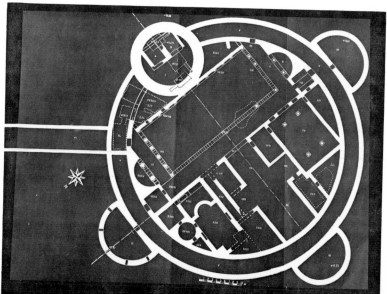

An aerial view of Herodium after excavation

The synagogue at Herodium. The synagogue was built during the First Revolt and must have been re-used in Bar-Kokhba's times

The excavations found proof of occupation of the site not only during the First Revolt but, most important to our subject, also during the Second Revolt, i.e. the Bar-Kokhba Revolt. The Bar-Kokhba warriors settled on the ruins of the palace, destroyed in the war of 66–70, and perhaps even re-used the synagogue which was erected there in the First Revolt. This synagogue is very similar to the only other synagogue known from the First Temple period – the one found at Masada. Many coins of Bar-Kokhba, as well as some inscribed sherds (*ostraca*) were found in the ruins.

186

Capitals of columns re-used to make benches in the synagogue at Herodium. A similar re-use of material was found in the synagogue at Masada

The excavations directed by Father R. de Vaux at Khirbet Qumran – the communal building of the sect of the Dead Sea Scrolls, several miles north of Murabba'at – proved that during the Bar-Kokhba Revolt there was some settlement on the ruined site, or to be more precise, the few Bar-Kokhba coins, found mainly on the surface of these ruins, suggested that at a certain time some insurgents may have used the ruins of the once fortified building as a military post. This has led *a priori* to the deduction by some scholars that the great ruins of the naturally fortified Masada,

Qumran and Masada

The tower at the corner of the communal building at Qumran

further south of En-gedi, had also been used by the fighters of Bar-Kokhba, an assumption that was apparently strengthened by the contents of one of the documents of Wadi Murabba'at.

The document, a bill of divorcement, is dated 'on the first of Marheshvan Year Six, at Masada'. In it 'Yehoseph son of Naqsan from . . . [missing] residing in Masada' divorces his wife, Miriam, daughter of Yehonathan from the Nablata, residing in Masada. Since the *era* of the dating is not mentioned, Milik – the scholar who published the document – assumed it to be the era of Provincia Arabia, which began at AD 106, i.e. the document was written in AD 112 at Masada. Milik thought that it belonged to a Jewish family who lived in Masada at that time side by side with the Roman garrison which was left there after the site's capture in AD 73. However, our excavations at Masada from 1963–5 revealed not one coin of Bar-Kokhba amongst the five thousand coins discovered

there, and from the level of the Roman garrison nothing was found which could be associated with Jewish families. It seems to me, therefore, that the unspecified era on the deed refers to the First Revolt. The silver coins of the First Revolt bear dates ranging from Year One to Year Five, in which Jerusalem and the Temple were destroyed. But possibly the people of Masada, who went on living there even after the fall of Jerusalem, must have reckoned according to the same era. In that case the divorce was given in Masada in AD 71–2 and the owner of the deed must have left the site before its fall in AD 73. The fact that a deed of the First Revolt should be found in Murabba'at need not surprise us. Among the many documents found there, there are some of earlier periods, including an Aramaic document bearing the clear date: 'Year Two of Neron Caesar', i.e. AD 55–6.

Since we mentioned the various sites in which remains from

A model of the Qumran complex showing the numerous cisterns and ritual baths (in blue). The model is in the Masada Museum

A rare silver shekel of the First Revolt dated Year Five found at Masada (AD 70)

left An aerial view of Masada, looking towards the south, showing part of the Roman siege camps and siege wall (bottom right) and the huge earthen assault ramp

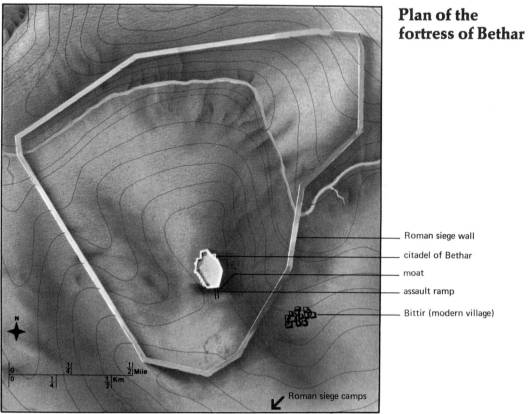

Plan of the fortress of Bethar

Roman siege wall

citadel of Bethar

moat

assault ramp

Bittir (modern village)

N

0	¼	½	Mile
0	¼	½	Km

Roman siege camps

Bar-Kokhba were found, it is fitting to conclude this short survey with Bethar, which was where Bar-Kokhba made his last stand and where he died. The site has not been excavated but the surface remains have been studied by various scholars, including Schulten, who also surveyed Masada, Reifenberg and Yeivin.

Bethar had been a city during the First Temple period, as attested by the Greek version of Joshua 15:59. The actual remains – mainly from Bar-Kokhba's times – lie north-west of an Arab village, eleven kilometres south-west of Jerusalem, on the main railroad to Tel-Aviv. The village, to this day, has preserved the ancient name with only a slight change to Bittir. The area with the ruins is called by the villagers: Khirbet el Yahud, i.e. 'the Jewish ruins'. The hill on which the fortress of Bethar stood is protected by nature; it is seven hundred metres above sea level; it is surrounded by a deep canyon on the east, west and north sides, and in the south, where it is connected by a saddle to the main ridge of mountains, there is a moat, five metres deep, fifteen metres wide and eighty metres long. The main fortified core comprises about twenty-five acres, and the circumference of its walls is about one thousand metres. The walls are very dilapidated but enough remains to reconstruct its plan: a hastily built wall with semi-circular bastions. Here and there one can discern earlier fortifications (square towers) mainly from the Hasmonaean and Herodian periods. The remains of the tremendous Roman efforts to besiege and capture the fort are also visible, mainly from aerial photographs. The whole area is surrounded by a siege wall (*circumvallatio*) not unlike the one in Masada, with a circumference of about four thousand metres. Furthermore, the remains of the assault ramp built in the moat are clearly visible. Two main siege camps are discernible in the aerial photographs, lying south-west of the ruins. The bigger of these two measures 400 by 200 metres and could have accommodated a legion; the other, 200 by 120 metres, would hold half a legion. Smaller camps are scattered in the vicinity. Some details in the construction of the camps' gates are reminiscent of the camp above the Cave of Letters, mentioned in Chapter 4.

Finally, we know some of the Roman units which took part in Bethar's siege from a badly preserved inscription, cut in the rock near the spring: *Leg V Mac et XI Cl* – that is, units of the fifth Macedonica and eleventh Claudia Legions. The place where Bar-Kokhba met his doom is now land mainly covered with groves and gardens. If and when it is excavated it is certain to add to our still fragmentary knowledge of the last days of ancient Israel.

Bethar – the last stand

opposite A view of Bethar showing the moat and assault ramp

14 No stone unturned

The fact that the cache discovered by Yoseph Porath was in a rather shallow crevice camouflaged by medium-sized stones and not beneath one of the huge boulders, confirmed our suspicion that when the Bar-Kokhba people entered the cave, they found the floors of its centre and inner halls already strewn all over with gigantic boulders which had fallen from the ceiling in more ancient days. This meant that their treasures, if hidden, should be looked for in crevices and cracks between the existing boulders, and our efforts should not be wasted on moving immovable stones which obviously the Bar-Kokhba people too could not have shifted. So we decided to change our work methods. We sent more people to search the innermost hall, although it had already been examined at least three times: first by the Bedouins, then by the 1953 expedition and lastly by us the previous year. This time the orders were: 'Do not leave any stone unturned that can be moved by two or three people.' Each team, therefore, was allocated a strip of the hall, starting from its entrance, and the method proved successful. From then on almost every day brought some new discovery; but from the tremendous amount of finds we made, I would not want to give the impression that every minute yielded something; some days we worked for many hours without finding anything.

Soon after the beginning of this new work method, not far away from the crevice of the letters, under a few medium-sized stones and within a rather thick layer of bats' dung – two iron knives were found lying on top of each other and nearby two spindle whorls. Close by these, Sefi found a coin lying on one of the stones and it was easy to read its inscription: on one side 'Shimeon' near the depiction of a palm tree, and on the other side 'of the Freedom of Jerusalem' near a vine leaf. This fellow Sefi, who also found the big cache, had sharp eyes indeed! As before, the find of this coin galvanised all of us afresh. Such coins could be had for practically nothing in any antiquities' shop, but it is quite another matter to find one inside a cave.

A day or two later, one of the students of archaeology made a very interesting discovery not far from where the knives had been found, and again beneath a few smallish stones deliberately covering a crevice. Out of it came two cooking pots, typical of the period; one still covered by soot, but the other 'brand new'; it was quite clear that the people who brought it to the cave did not get a chance to use it. Near these pots lay what looked like a huge net, folded, rolled and tied. Even before opening it we thought this

The two sides of the second Bar-Kokhba coin found inside the cave (see also page 87). On one side is a date palm with the inscription in paleo-Hebrew 'Shimeon' and on the other is a grape leaf with the inscription 'of the Freedom of Jerusalem'

left The 'brand new' cooking pot; it
is typical of the Bar-Kokhba period
below The fowling net as it was found

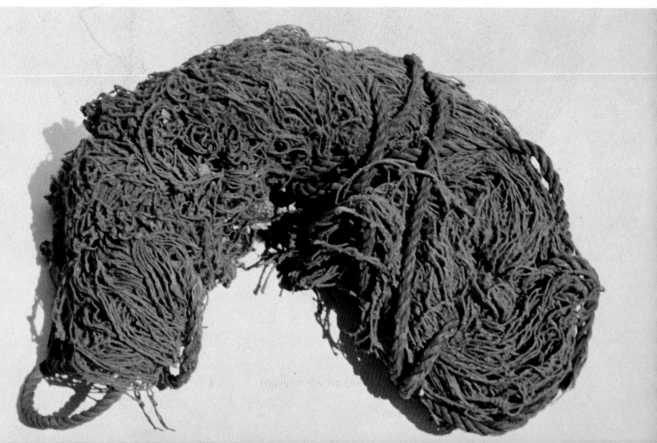

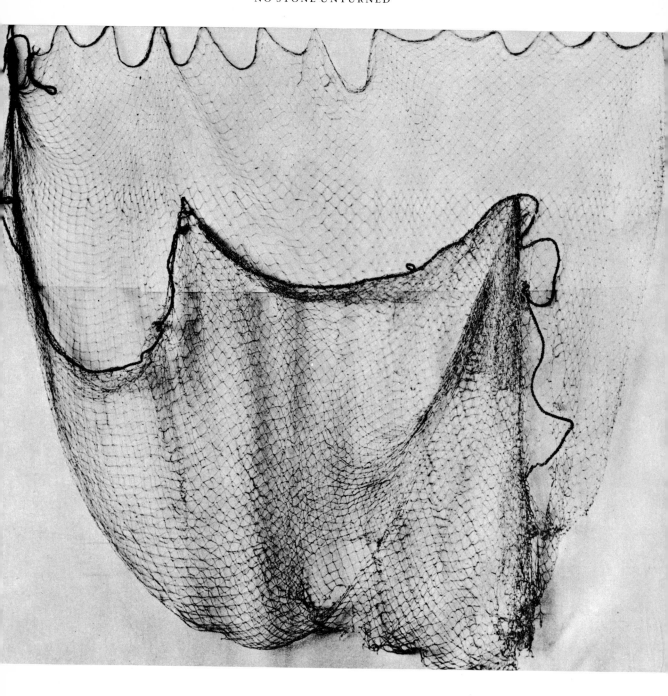

The fowling net when opened

net must have been made for bird-catching; after all, it was not very likely that it served to catch fish in the Dead Sea. . . . When the net was spread out in Jerusalem later, it turned out to be rather large: six by ten metres, and extremely well made. It was most probably made for fowling.

Next day we transferred one of the teams to examine a transitional area between halls B and C, and a few minutes after they began shifting some stones, one of the team rushed to call me with excited urgency: 'Come and see what I found!' A few metres to the right of the place where the big cache had been found, another crevice appeared between two boulders, covered on top by small stones. When these were removed, one could see that there lay in the bottom of the crevice a bunch of six keys, some small and one big, with a handle twenty centimetres long. These keys, together with those found the previous year, formed the biggest key collection of that type ever found, and the fact that the six belonged to one bunch enables us to study better the tiny differences between them. The big key may have been that of a citadel or public building in En-gedi, and again the very fact that the refugees took the keys with them into hiding, indicates that they expected to come back and use them, not believing that their end was imminent. The keys are all of the toothed type, their teeth fitting into a bolt with a corresponding number of teeth that are pushed inward by spring when the key is inserted. Most of the keys had five teeth arranged in a uniform pattern, the difference between them being the varying length of the different elements of the arms. This type of key, very common in the Roman period, was called in the Mishna 'knee' or 'elbow' key, to tell it apart from the other type known as *gamma* keys. *Gamma* keys were nearer present-day keys in that the bit was attached directly to the shank and opened the lock by turning. Like many other of our finds dating to the times of the Mishna, the keys also helped us in better understanding some of the Mishnaic *Halakhoth*. For example in Kelim xiv: 8 we read: 'If a "knee-shaped" key is broken at its joint, it becomes insusceptible to uncleanness. R. Judah declares it is susceptible since one may still open from within. If a "*gamma*-shaped" key is broken off at its bend, it becomes insusceptible.' That is to say a *gamma* key which can be used only in the lock, is useless the moment the bit breaks off the shank. The bit of an elbow key on the other hand, even though separated from its shank, can still be used for opening the bolt from within. This is understandable, for a *gamma* key was turned on the axis of its shank and if this broke off there was no means of turning the bit within the lock. The broken part of an elbow key could be used from inside as there was no need for the shank which served only to pass the bit through the door from without. The tines, or teeth, could be introduced into the tumbler from within, thus releasing the bolt directly. Even the tiny ring

Yale keys – Roman style

overleaf The 'knee' or 'elbow' keys including the big key and the two tiny ring keys

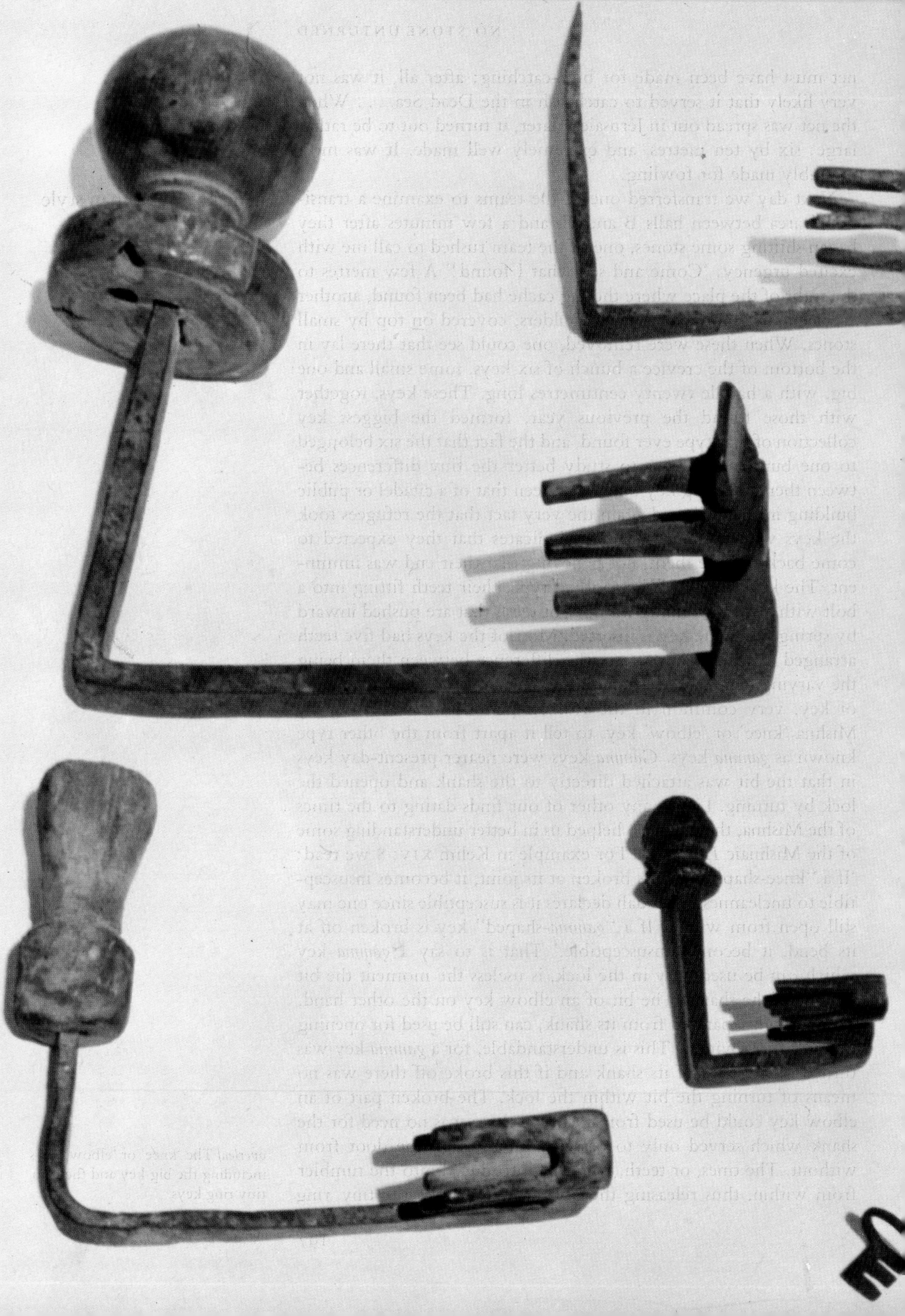

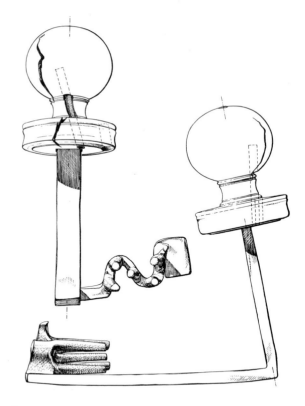

The big key and drawings of it showing technical details. The two parts of the shank are the upper arm and forearm. The bit is attached to the forearm and has several teeth. To open a door from the outside, it was pierced by a hole through which the key was inserted; after the door was locked it was impossible to move the bolt; this was held fast by a tumbler consisting of a number of prongs attached to a spring or a number of springs which forced them into holes penetrating the bolt. When the key was inserted into the lock, the forearm reached around the bolt and the bit engaged the tumbler, enabling the bolt to be pulled back out of the socket in the door jamb, using the entire key as a handle

keys, like the one found in the woman's cache in the basket, – most probably used to open jewellery boxes or the like – are mentioned in the Mishna. The ring had no part in the opening or closing of the lock; it was just a means of enabling the owner conveniently to carry it about at all times. We read for example in Tosefta, Shabbath, IV: 11: 'A woman shall not go out in public [on the Sabbath] with a key which is on [her] finger. If she does go out, it binds her to make a guilt offering.' In other words it was considered a tool.

Every expedition has one 'character' who works very hard and devotedly but seems never to find anything. We too had one such fellow amongst us. He was Haim, a member of Kibbutz Sa-sa in Galilee. The discovery of the keys was made in the morning. That same day, early in the afternoon, all of us began to show the customary symptoms of lethargy resulting from the shortage of oxygen. We lay on the huge stones of the front third of the inner hall, telling stories to one another to keep awake. Suddenly the head of Haim, looking like a chimney-sweep, emerged out of a crevice a few metres away from us.

'Yigael,' he said, 'I am desperate. I have just been crawling in a most promising crevice and I found nothing.'

We were all sorry for him; from the start he diligently crawled into every hole and cranny, sometimes spending hours in underground crevices and caverns, oblivious of activities in the rest of the cave, but he never made a find.

'I am desperate,' he said again; 'everybody discovers something except me!' But a few moments later I heard his voice shouting: 'Come quickly! I believe I have got something!' We all jumped towards him, our fatigue forgotten. Close by where he lay was a huge boulder, very familiar by then to all of us as one of the cave's landmarks. Under it we could discern a tiny horizontal crevice which miraculously had escaped our attention up to then. In that crevice, not very deep down, we could see a bundle of palm fibres and strings. At first it looked like another net. But when we removed it, it appeared to be round, about fifty centimetres in diameter, closely packed and pedantically tied. I could feel something hard inside but my imagination did not suffice to guess what lay in store for us: it was a set of three glass bowls, or platters, one large and two small. As the photographer was at that moment (as usual, it seemed) busy with another team, we very carefully carried the package back to camp. While doing so, we were again filled with admiration for the woman (it must have been a woman!) who packed it so well, and as one member of our team remarked: 'She not only packed it, but carried it from En-gedi, over the ledge, to this remote cave, without Mussa's rope ladder and assistance, and yet she did not break it!'

The palm fibre package tied with string in which the glass bowls were found

201

We opened the package later in the camp, in the presence of the Prime Minister, Mr David Ben-Gurion, who came to visit us that day. When we took out the plates we could scarcely believe our eyes. The glass was as translucent as if it had just been manufactured. I must confess that a terrible thought flashed through my mind that if I should find 'Made in Japan' stamped on the bowls I would collapse on the spot. Subconsciously I turned the bowl over, but there was no such inscription. It is common to see ancient glass with patina created by dust and humidity throughout the ages; in fact, we like ancient glass for that very reason. But here in the cave, because of the absolute lack of humidity, no patina formed and the glass was preserved exactly as it was two thousand years ago. The Romans always admired transparent and translucent glass. The large bowl was of particular beauty. It was manufactured by moulding, grinding and cutting. The circular facets contained within two thin lines, both on the centre of the underside and around the rim, are all *intaglio*. The edge has what is called a cut 'bead and bar' pattern. Overall rotary polishing is evident. The diameter of the bowl is 33.8 centimetres, and the thickness of the glass is between three and four millimetres. Although glassware of similar

opposite The large glass bowl: note the round facets and the cut rim
below The large bowl and one of the small plates photographed in the camp after the package had been unwrapped

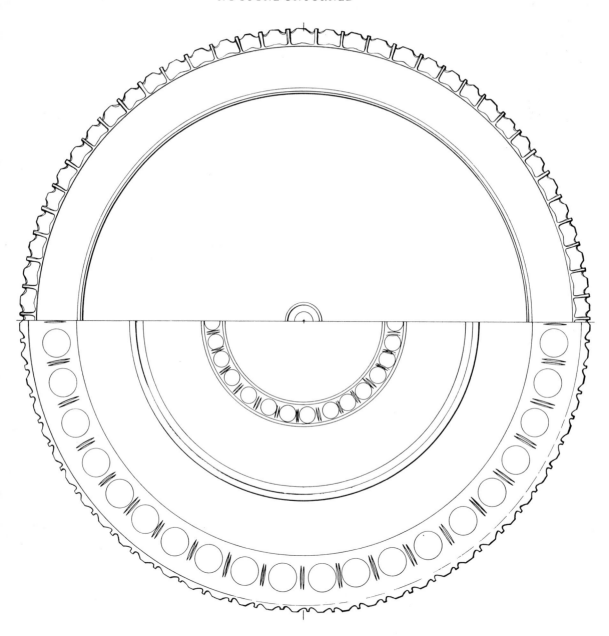

Drawings of the large bowl showing
its inside (upper half of drawing) and
outside, and a side view

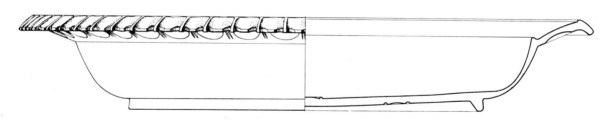

technique from the Roman Empire is known, no complete specimen of that type has yet been found anywhere within its vast area. After I published a photograph of the bowl in a preliminary article in the *Illustrated London News*, I received a letter from Miss Dorothy Charlesworth – a British archaeologist and an expert on glass – in which she wrote *inter alia*: 'I have a fragment of a rim exactly the same as this, found at Richborough, Kent, and now preserved in the museum there. I know of nothing like it in Britain and elsewhere in Western Europe within the Roman Empire.' Miss Charlesworth sent me a drawing and a photograph of the fragment from Richborough and a reconstruction of the complete plate. From it it looks not only similar, but the possibility should not be disregarded that the two bowls were actually manufactured in the same workshop. Strange are the ways of history! One bowl finds its way to a remote cave in the Judaean Desert, and the other to Kent in England. But at that time, after all, the whole area was one Roman common market! This beautiful set of glass must have been used on special occasions, Sabbath or holidays. It is doubtful whether the people in the cave had any opportunity to use it at all and so they buried it safely in the crevice under the rock, where it remained for 1,800 years until Haim of Kibbutz Sa-sa unearthed it.

One of the small glass plates

A less exciting discovery – albeit quite important scientifically – was made again in the inner hall, not far away from the crevice of the letters. One of the volunteers picked up on the surface a cylindrical-shaped basket made of willows. Its sides had become coated with a thick layer of bat droppings, which is why it looked just like a stone and had hitherto passed unnoticed. This new find enriched our already varied and ample collection of baskets and mats. The study of the technique of basketry is a fascinating sub-ject. I remember that while I was studying them, I consulted

A side view of the willow basket or *cista*

one of the expert basketmakers in Israel today, a Druse from a village in Galilee. He was shown some of these baskets without being told their provenance or age. He looked at them very carefully and then said:

'These baskets must be very old.'

'How can you tell?' he was asked, and he replied without hesitation:

'Whoever made these baskets did not cheat in the basketry. This is honest craftsmanship, so it must be old.'

A view of the bottom of the willow basket

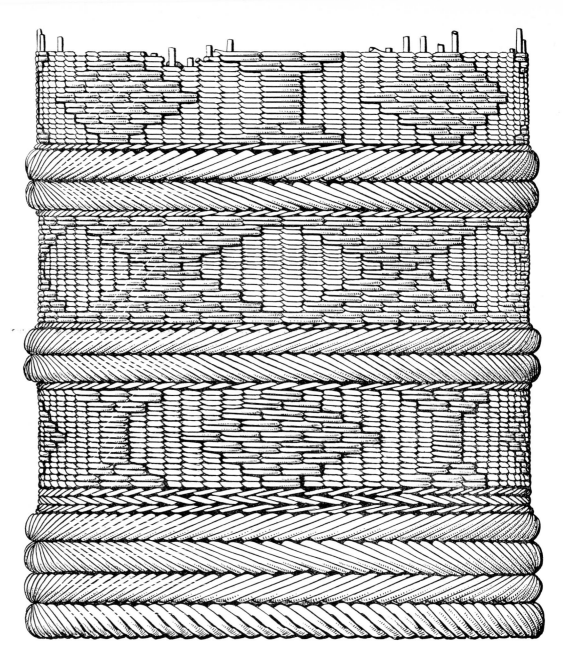

A detailed drawing of the willow basket showing its patterns

The newly-found cylindrical willow basket was even more intricate in its technique than those I had shown to the Druse. Later on I met in England Miss Dorothy Wright – one of the leading experts on basketry and author of several books on the subject – who was of great help to me; but even she was slightly baffled by the technique of that particular basket and therefore consulted several willow makers. In a letter to me she wrote: 'I took the photographs to one of the best willow workers in the country and he said . . . he hoped no one should ever ask him to make such a very difficult basket! He admired it very much.'

As already mentioned, we began the new season by clearing the second or eastern entrance to the first hall. The passage between these two was blocked by stones, and our purpose was twofold. First, this entrance like the western entrance, must have been used by the cave's inmates not only as an observation post, but also a great deal as a terrace for relaxation, where air and light were more abundant than in the inside of the cave, and we hoped to find there remnants of food and traces of daily use. Second, I wished to have another exit from the cave for security reasons. We did not feel very comfortable knowing that the only exit from

The basket in which the woman's cache was found (see also page 145)

The mat as found in the burial niche and (*below*) the same mat after cleaning

that cave was through the one bending, vertical crevice at the end of the tunnel in the western entrance. Even those of us who were not prone to claustrophobia always felt that it was rather dangerous. And in fact, several days after we finished clearing the second entrance and opened it to the main cave, something happened to prove that we were wise just in time. Now that we were sure of having a second outlet, I detailed a few soldiers to remove some boulders in the first entrance in order to widen that narrow crevice through which we had to crawl every time we entered the cave. While they were working, one of the large boulders, weighing several hundred pounds, came loose, slid and completely blocked the entrance; we stood there speechless. It was nearly impossible to move that stone, but the rays of light which penetrated through the other newly-cleared passage were reassuring indeed.

Regards from . . . the Bedouins

In order to facilitate the work on the second, eastern, entrance, we put up another rope ladder from the outside and could then enter it directly. Originally there must have been a direct passage between this entrance and the main cave, but now the floor there was littered with huge stones which made even crawling between the two most difficult. The team that worked here, since they had

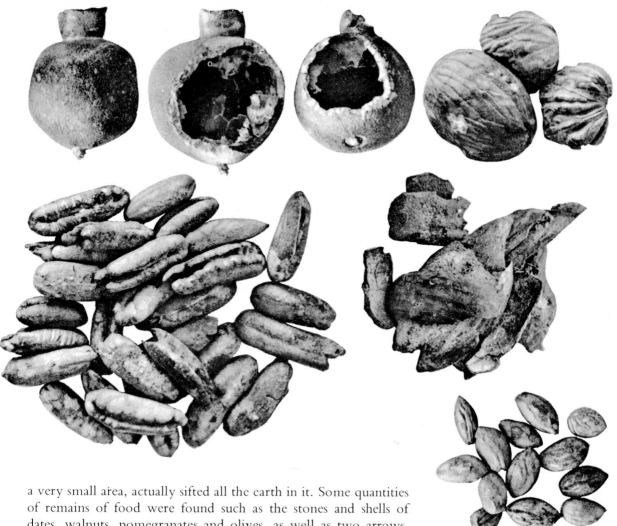

a very small area, actually sifted all the earth in it. Some quantities of remains of food were found such as the stones and shells of dates, walnuts, pomegranates and olives, as well as two arrows. However, in addition they found two small fragments of written documents: one on papyrus and the other on parchment. Although they were small, they were very significant indeed. These two pieces must have fallen from the hands of the ransacking Bedouins, who probably used this second entrance to sort their loot before they departed from the cave. The papyrus fragment was an important link between the activities of the Bedouins and some of the documents published in Jordan. It was written in Nabataean, and after careful study it turned out to be part of a Nabataean document which had been published in 1954 by the French scholar, Father J. Starcky, without any mention of its exact provenance. He indicated only that it was discovered by Bedouins near the Dead Sea together with other documents dating to the Bar-Kokhba period. This seemed to suggest that some of the documents originated in our cave. Other documents, we now know, came from the Cave of Horrors, as indicated by some fragments of the Minor Prophets, found there by Aharoni's expedition. These fragments belong to

Samples of food found mainly in the entrances to the cave: pomegranates, nuts, olives and date stones

overleaf A team at work in hall A which was completely excavated

211

The tiny fragment of a scroll on which verses seven and eight of Numbers 20 were preserved

the group published by Father D. Barthélemy in 1953, as coming from an 'unknown source'.

The tiny parchment fragment discovered in the second entrance fortunately preserved some Hebrew words, enough to recognise it as verses seven and eight of Chapter 20 of the Book of Numbers:

'And the Lord said to Moses, Take the rod and assemble the congregation, you and Aaron your brother, and tell the rock before their eyes to yield its waters; so you shall bring water out of the rock for them; so you shall give drink to the congregation and their cattle.'

It was the second fragment of a Biblical text which we discovered, the first having been Psalms 15, found in the previous season.

Water in the desert

The waters from the rock encountered in the tiny fragment from the Book of Numbers was not the only water coming our way

Watching a rare waterfall in Nahal Hever, west of the Cave of Letters

that day. When we climbed back to camp to examine the finds of the day – it was already rather late in the afternoon – we suddenly heard a roaring noise from the direction of the canyon of Nahal Hever. Simultaneously we heard shouts of joy from members of our team who ran through the camp, shouting: 'Water in Nahal Hever! A flood in Nahal Hever!' The skies above were blue and we could not see even a tiny cloud. We ran to the brink of the precipice and got there just when tons of gushing water from the west had reached our area. The water was the result of heavy rains that fell several hours earlier inland, near Hebron and other parts of the country, while we in the desert had enjoyed a beautiful dry day. We hurried further west, about one kilometre closer to the Cave of Horrors, for a better view. Up to that time we had been familiar only with the 'dry' waterfalls, that is to say the huge rock-steps over which flash flood-water fell, but we had never seen them filled. When we got there the sun had nearly set, and we just managed to get a last, breath-taking view as we lay on a bluff above the chasm. Incredible quantities of water mixed with earth swept down towards the bottom of the canyon, as if coming from nowhere. We stayed there till late that evening, seeing nothing more in the darkness, but enjoying the deafening noise of the falling water. Even the great excitement caused by the discoveries of the day were somewhat overshadowed by this phenomenon of nature. At dinner-time one of the older volunteers – whose son, incidentally, was with one of the other teams – opened the Bible and asked one of the girls to read aloud from II Kings 3:16–17 and 20, which described the battle of Yehoram, King of Israel and Yehoshaphat, King of Judah, against Moab, and in which the desert near the Dead Sea, not far away from where we sat, had no water:

'And he said, Thus says the Lord, I will make this dry stream-bed full of pools. For thus says the Lord, You shall not see wind or rain, but that stream-bed shall be filled with water, so that you shall drink, you, your cattle, and your beasts. . . . The next morning, about the time of offering the sacrifice, behold, water came from the direction of Edom, till the country was filled with water.'

15 'He who toils shall find'

I have described the most important discoveries made in our cave. It so happened that the other teams were less fortunate as far as discoveries were concerned, although they worked just as diligently in the most difficult conditions. It was really heart-breaking to see the volunteers trying so hard and endangering themselves, always to find that the Bedouins had somehow preceded them. However, I should like to describe one discovery made in Nahal Mishmar, by team C headed by Bar-Adon. Although it has no connection with Bar-Kokhba, it is significant that it was made in a cave in which remains of the Bar-Kokhba fugitives were also found. It was a find belonging to men seeking shelter thousands of years earlier. These desert caves seem always to have served as a refuge place for stricken people. I have already expressed my admiration for the tenacity of Bar-Adon, who decided to return to his cave in the second season despite the fact that no spectacular finds were made there in the first. And indeed, the first week of the second season was no different. Small finds were made, but again it was quite obvious that the Bedouins had been there first. Then on Tuesday, 21 March, the very day that we discovered the keys and the set of glass, a turning point occurred. As our sages have said: 'He who toils shall find.'

Late that afternoon the telephone buzzed in our cave and the excited voice of Bar-Adon told me that at two o'clock they had discovered a big cache of metal objects in a crevice in the cave hidden by a slanting stone. They had not yet opened it, but could see quite clearly hundreds – he repeated the word 'hundreds' – of objects wrapped in a mat. I congratulated him and was convinced at that moment that what he had found was similar to what we found in the first season in the first hall, namely a cache of Roman metal objects, though probably bigger than ours. As evening was near, Bar-Adon postponed the recording and photography of the objects to the following morning. What happened then is best described by Joseph Aviram who was present to witness the exciting occasion: 'Early in the morning we went to camp C. When we arrived in the cave, Bar-Adon and his team were already sitting near the cache, busy betting and speculating concerning its nature. In high spirits they waited for a sign that they might begin to take out the objects, which was given to them after everything had been properly photographed. Bar-Adon was sitting in the centre and each object he took out was immediately passed from hand to hand, admired by everyone and exclamations of joy abounded on

Bar-Adon, leader of team C, at work in Nahal Mishmar

opposite Some of the 240 copper mace-heads found in the 'Cave of Treasure' in Nahal Mishmar

217

all sides, prompted not only by the beauty of the objects but also
by the quantity of them. Three and a half hours of very high tension thus went by, during which all sorts of theories were tendered
by those present. Suddenly someone exclaimed: "The Holy
Vessels of the Temple!" and spontaneously everyone started
singing a very well-known Hebrew song of the Temple. Another
member, watching an object which looked like a standard shaped
like an eagle, declared without hesitation: "A Roman [standard's]
eagle fell into the hands of Bar-Kokhba!" '

And indeed, later in the day, rumours had reached our caves,
through telephones and visitors, that Bar-Adon's find was possibly
nothing less than the Holy Vessels of the Temple. One visitor even

Some of the eighty tubular objects with spiral ornaments found in the Nahal Mishmar cave

mentioned the candelabrum. It sounded incredible, but then so many incredible things had been happening lately that everyone was prepared to accept and believe anything; the atmosphere of the desert is known to affect the imagination and inspire people with all sorts of fantasies, now as in the days of yore.

When the day's work was over in the various sectors, the heads of the teams went to visit Bar-Adon in his camp, where he laid out an exhibition of his treasures. We were staggered by what we saw: hundreds of metal objects, some of them extremely curious, some of them very beautiful indeed. Altogether 429 objects, amongst them 240 differently shaped mace-heads of copper, about 20 chisels and axes of various shapes and sizes, 80 tube-like objects bearing

Three thousand years before Bar-Kokhba

219

strange and interesting spiral ornaments, 5 sickle-shaped objects made of hippopotamus ivory, and 10 beautiful, extraordinary round copper stands, some of them bearing moulded birds and other patterns. After careful examination all of us came to the conclusion that this cache had no relation to Bar-Kokhba and was probably three thousand years older, from the so-called Chalcolithic period. This was more dramatic evidence supporting what was already known from excavations in Murabba'at and our own caves, namely that thousands of years before Bar-Kokhba other refugees also found shelter in these remote caves. But such a treasure of that early period, the transition between the Stone Age and the Copper Age, so beautifully made and of such high quality, had never been found before in Israel. Its dating in the Chalcolithic period was made on the basis of similarities between some of the elements depicted on the objects, and those known from other sites of that period, although not in metal. This conclusion was later authenticated when Bar-Adon submitted the mat in which the objects were wrapped to Carbon 14 tests. These confirmed that they were five thousand years old.

Where did these objects come from? Quite obviously they could not have been made on the spot. One theory was that they actually originated from a Chalcolithic temple in En-gedi, of which remains have for a long time been known to exist high above the plateau near the rich water source. It is true that many of the objects were of clear cultic significance. This possibility was one of the reasons that prompted Professor B. Mazar, excavator of En-gedi, to excavate that temple a few years later. A very interesting temple was indeed found there, but alas, no objects of metal, which led one member of the expedition to suggest – more seriously than in jest – that this was proof indeed that the objects did after all come from the temple, where nothing remained. The question still remains: what prompted these people to flee to the caves? We know what caused the Bar-Kokhba people to seek shelter there, but who were these Chalcolithic people, and why would they – three thousand years earlier – take refuge in these caves? Perhaps we shall never know. One possibility seems to be that they fled into the caves as a result of the conquest of Palestine by the first Pharaohs, who – as attested by other archaeological excavations – had by then penetrated the Negev. Whatever the case, it was quite puzzling to encounter but two layers in most of these caves: Chalcolithic of 3000 BC, and directly on it and sometimes mingled with it, the remains of Bar-Kokhba: two remote periods, two different people – but the same caves in which remains waited for the spade.

But let us come back to Bar-Kokhba and our cave. It is now time to discuss what was found in the huge bundle of papyri discovered on the first day of the second season.

opposite A copper stand of the Chalcolithic period found in the Nahal Mishmar cave

The origin of the cult objects

16 The life and trials of Babata

The largest cache of documents found in the Cave of Letters was the archive of Babata, daughter of Shimeon son of Menahem. Thanks to this woman – who managed to survive two husbands and must have spent most of her life in litigation, either suing the guardians of her fatherless son or being sued by the various members of her deceased husbands' families – we have come by a priceless source for the period just preceding the war of Bar-Kokhba. It is full of legal, historical, geographical and linguistic data.

Babata's habit – typical of many even in our days – of never discarding any slip of paper in her possession, and her meticulous and orderly nature, are responsible for the fact that all her documents, thirty-five in number, were found neatly packed and 'filed' by subject-matter. Her archive has disclosed to us more about her private life than she might have wanted us to know, but

The unopened archive of Babata; note how securely it is packed and tied with rope

222

since the publication of these details cannot harm her any more I hope we shall be forgiven.

Babata's documents, as already mentioned, were found in a leather pouch, wrapped in sacking and tied together with twisted ropes. Several of the papyri were badly damaged by worms and moths, but most of the documents were remarkably well preserved.

Although the bundle with Babata's archive was sent to Jerusalem in the care of my wife and Art Buchwald during my stay in the field, I specifically requested my wife not to hand it over to Bieberkraut before my return to Jerusalem. I wanted to witness the actual opening of the parcel in order to see for myself how it was packed, and to make sure that every phase of the opening be properly photographed and recorded. On Wednesday, 29 March, at noon, a day after our return to Jerusalem, I went without delay to Bieberkraut with the package. By then I already knew that the earlier gnawing fear at the back of my mind lest the package consist of nothing but empty papyri – i.e. writing material – was groundless. That same morning Mr D. Harris photographed the bundle at my home and while handling it I could quite clearly detect traces of letters on the fringe of many of the documents.

A view of one end of the unopened archive with the ends of the bundles of documents visible

left Removing the archive from its box in preparation for the opening *opposite* Professor Bieberkraut begins to open the archive with his wife looking on

At 5.30 p.m. we began the opening procedure. The papyri seemed to be packed and tied fourfold: first each papyrus separately; then groups of papyri in special bundles; then the whole batch within the leather pouch; and lastly the whole pouch in the sacking. The sight of the heap of papyri, once the pouch had been removed, was thrilling indeed. It was the largest single collection of ancient documents ever found in the Holy Land. It was vital to keep the bundles separate before proceeding to open them, but Bieberkraut had no suitable boxes for this purpose at his home. I therefore rushed out to the nearby market, searching in vain for some kind of shop that sold boxes. What happened there is worth recounting since it illustrates how everybody, even simple shopkeepers, were carried away by the discoveries in the Bar-Kokhba caves. In desperation I entered a general store and asked for boxes. The shopkeeper had no empty ones at hand, but he turned his shop upside down, emptying others of their contents, until he finally collected the necessary assortment of sizes and shapes. I had not made mention of the purpose of my errand, nor did I introduce myself, but when I wanted to pay him, he said: 'No charge! Let this be my contribution to operation Bar-Kokhba.' He must have recognised me and guessed correctly.

The leather purse which contained the documents, after opening, and (*below*) drawings of the purse showing how it was originally folded and sewn

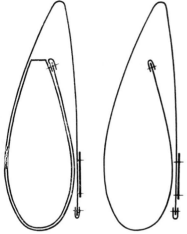

The opened archive showing the separate bundles of documents

On examining the unopened papyri I noticed that their state of preservation varied, and so I decided that Bieberkraut should start by unrolling those that were better preserved. Accordingly we numbered them from 1 to 35 by their state of preservation, which does not in any way indicate their chronological order.

Passover was approaching, and since Bieberkraut had made previous arrangements to spend the holiday outside Jerusalem, I was compelled most reluctantly to postpone the actual unfolding for several days. On Wednesday, 5 April, the first three big papyri were unrolled and flattened. A glance at them showed immediately that they differed from the batch of deeds of the Bar-Kokhba period already described in Chapter 10. Not only were some of them written in Greek, but one of them clearly bore the date: 'Year Fourteen of Hadrian' – i.e. AD 130, that is to say preceding the Bar-Kokhba Revolt.

I was fortunate later to find in my erstwhile teacher and colleague, Professor J. Polotsky, the famous Egyptologist and linguist, a collaborator who undertook the deciphering of the Greek papyri. Much of what is told in the following lines is due to his painstaking work.

Due to the fact that the papyri were opened without regard to their date or contents, it took us considerable time to grasp the intricate contents of the various documents and their relation to one another. The following description of their contents, therefore, will not be according to the order of their opening, but according to their dates.

Altogether there were thirty-five documents: six in Nabataean, three in Aramaic, seventeen in Greek, and nine in Greek with subscriptions and signatures in Aramaic or Nabataean. These documents belonged to Babata and her family and dealt with matters of property and with law-suits brought by and against her. Before dealing separately with the contents of the most important papyri, it is worth discussing three main subjects, which will enable the reader to follow more closely the detailed discoveries.

Twenty-three out of the thirty-five documents belonged to the type commonly known as 'double deeds', or to use the Talmudic usage, 'tied deeds'. The use of 'tied deeds' is a very old and known practice of the ancient world; but since our documents are so well preserved and include even Nabataean 'tied deeds' which are some-what different, a short description of them will acquaint the reader with this strange way of deed-writing in some of its best preserved specimens. This system was used, of course, for the more important documents.

The original deed was first written on the upper part of a papy-rus sheet (*scriptura interior*), usually in a small, particularly cursive script. Then the scribe left a blank space of about one inch (varying according to the size of the particular deed) and again wrote the whole deed (*scriptura exterior*), usually verbatim, in a large and clear hand. Next he rolled the upper part of the deed, including the gap between its two sections. This part of the deed was then tied with a thread which ran vertically down the front of the fold, pierced the document, was knotted and was then drawn diagonally across the back to make a second knot and so forth to the end. The witnesses signed their names on the back (the *verso*), each next to one knot. Their signatures ran from the knots towards the lower end of the deed at right angles to the lines drawn on the outer section (*exterior*) of the document adjoining the *interior*. After this, the deed was

opposite Three bundles of documents as they were found. The documents in each bundle deal with one subject only

'Tied deeds'

Part of the back of a 'tied deed' showing the method of tying and the position of the signatures

opposite Schematic drawings of a
'tied deed': (*a*) The *interior*, still
unrolled and tied. (*b*) The *interior*
opened. (*c*) The back of *a*; note the
signatures. (*d*) The back of *b*

again rolled up but left untied. The object of this procedure was to
safeguard the original deed from falsification, while at the same
time to enable its holder to use the lower *exterior* half for daily
reference as required. In case of doubt, and only then, the *interior*
could be opened in the appropriate office. In some cases, but not
in Babata's archive, the impressions of the witnesses' seals were
attached to the knots. This procedure prevented turning each part
of the double deed into what is called a 'simple' deed by tearing
the deed horizontally into two. Further means to prevent this
were observed in the Nabataean, Jewish and Aramaic deeds in
Babata's archive as follows: the scribe began writing the text of
the *interior* on the back of the document at the bottom, then turned
it over and continued his work on the front. In this way some
writing appeared on the back of the *interior* part of the document
to prove that it was not a simple document, written on one side
only. The number of signatures corresponds to that of the ties,
usually five or seven. This includes the signature of the giver of the
deed – the one who undertakes the obligation – which usually
appears above the signatures of the witnesses and near the first tie
in the form: 'Shimeon son of Menahem, in person', whereas those
of the witnesses are written, for example, as: 'Yehoseph son of
Hananiah, witness'. The witnesses sign in their own language and
writing: the Jews in Aramaic or Greek; the Nabataeans in Nabataean, etc. In Talmudic literature there are numerous references to
the 'tied deed' and particularly how to prevent its turning into a
'simple deed'. Most of these allusions fit admirably the type of
deed that we discovered; moreover, the Talmud and our deeds
advance mutual understanding. Some quotations will suffice: 'A
simple deed – its witnesses [signatures] are in the front, and a tied
one – its witnesses [signatures] on its back. A simple one with
signatures on its back – a tied one with its signatures in the front –
both are null and void. R. Hananiah son of Gamaliel says: A tied
[deed] in which the signatures are in front is legal, since it can be
turned into a simple one. Rabban Shimeon son of Gamaliel says:
All [these rules] is subject to State Law [i.e. the non-Jewish law]'
(Mishna, Babba Batra x:1).

It is also worth mentioning the Babylonian Talmud (Baba
Batra 160b): 'If the tied deed has many knots, the number of the
witnesses should be increased accordingly', otherwise the deed
will be a 'bald one'; 'Which is a bald one? The one in which the
number of the knots surpass the number of the witnesses' (Mishna
Gittin viii:10).

And lastly it is interesting to quote Rav Yirmiyah, there, about
the location of the witnesses' signatures in the tied deed. 'At the
back of the written side, and in right-angle direction to the writing
– outside', exactly as is the procedure in the documents which we
discovered.

a

b

c

d

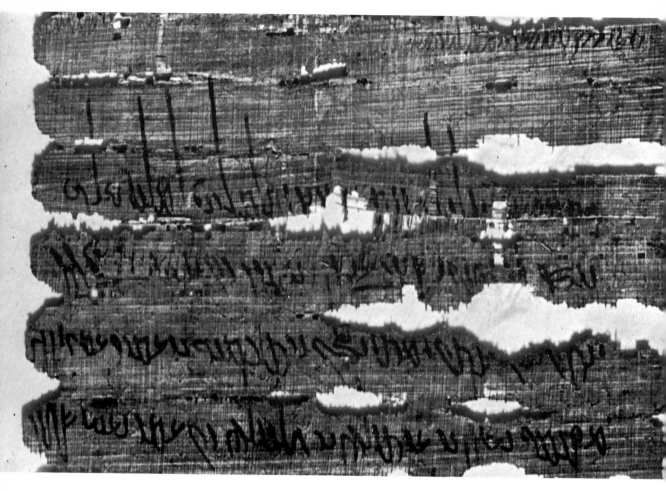

The top of a Nabataean document, partially eaten away by a moth. The date is: 'On the eighth of Elul in the twenty-third year of Rabael the king, King of the Nabataeans, who maintained life and brought deliverance to his people' (AD 93). (For further details see p. 235)

The Nabataean documents – all from the end of the first century AD, when the Nabataeans were still semi-autonomous and had their own kings – are dated according to the regnal year of the Nabataean monarchs. All the other documents are later than AD 106 at which time Trajan dissolved the Nabataean kingdom, and created instead the Roman Provincia Arabia. Since most of these deeds were drawn up by the official clerks of the Romans, they are dated by three methods: the regnal year of Hadrian; the civil year (from January to December) of Rome (named after the consuls of that year) with Roman months and days; and lastly according to the era of the Arabian Province (beginning at AD 106) with the Aramaic months rendered usually by their Greek (Macedonian) equivalents. Thus a typical Greek document of 12 October AD 125 would read as follows:

'In the ninth year of Imperator Traianus Hadrianus Caesar Augustus, in the consulship of M. Valerius Asiaticus II and Titius Aquilinus, IV Id. October [i.e. four days before the ides of October], and according to the era of the Provincia Arabia twentieth year, on the twenty-fourth of the month of Hyperberetaius which is called Tishri.'

This system of dating, coupled with a great number of documents bearing the regnal years of Hadrian (a custom more popular in the Orient than in Rome, whose dating was by the emperor's tribunal power years), which lasted over a period of eleven years, enables us to understand precisely the system of the regnal years; in fact one document enables us also to fix more exactly the beginning of Hadrian's tribunal power years. These documents which were, as a rule, drawn up in the office of the Roman governors of the Province, reveal names of three previously unknown governors of the Province. Moreover, our documents make a modest addition to the name-list of the consuls of Rome, quite an unexpected contribution by our Babata to the knowledge of Roman history. . . .

Method of dating

The life story of Babata's own family as well as that of her two husbands is complicated. To understand the contents of her documents and refrain from unnecessary repetition, let us now present a genealogical table of Babata's family.

Dramatis personae

Babata's father, Shimeon son of Menahem, and her mother, Miriam daughter of Yehoseph son of Menashe, lived in Mahoza, a town at the southern end of the Dead Sea in the Nabataean region. Shimeon endowed his wife Miriam with all his possessions during his lifetime, and after her death these passed on to Babata.

Babata's first husband was a certain Yeshua son of Yehoseph. We know very little about him. The main subject of some of the documents, though, is his and Babata's son, who after Yeshua's death is referred to as the 'Orphan Yeshua son of Yeshua'.

The family of Khthusion forms the link connecting all the others. It was a large family that came originally from En-gedi. After the death of her first husband, Babata married Yehudah Khthusion son of Eleazar, an inhabitant of En-gedi, who had taken up residence in Mahoza. This Yehudah died almost immediately after the wedding, leaving to Babata a large property, claimed by his relatives to have belonged mainly to his father, the founder of the family, Eleazar son of Yehudah Khthusion.

The family of Be'ayan is the key to our understanding how Babata found her way to, and eventual death in, the Cave of Letters, where the family of Yehonathan ben Be'ayan, the leader of En-gedi (as we have learned from the letters), took refuge. Yehudah, Babata's second husband, had – before his marriage to her – already been married to another woman from En-gedi, none other than Miriam, daughter of Be'ayan and apparently the sister of Yehonathan, En-gedi's commander. By this first wife, Yehudah seems to have had a daughter named Shelamzion ('Peace of Zion').

The family of Kimber: Shelamzion, Miriam's daughter, was

married before the death of her father Yehudah, to a man from another En-gedi family named Yehudah son of Hananiah son of Somala, who, as shown by their marriage certificate, was known as Kimber. This same Shelamzion inherited a certain amount of property in En-gedi from her father, and the guardians of her uncle's (Yeshua son of Eleazar) orphans also gave up part of the orphans' property to her.

This complicated genealogy can best be visualised with the aid of the following table:

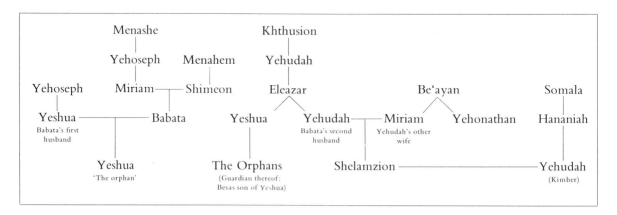

Many surprises awaited us in the Cave of Letters; the biggest of course was the discovery of Bar-Kokhba's letters, although the search for documents was the primary objective of the expedition. But even in our wildest dreams we did not expect to find documents which would shed new light on the little known history and language of the Nabataeans and their land, which from AD 106 onwards became the Provincia Arabia.

The Nabataeans – whose capital was that fantastic rock-city Petra – were Semites of Arab stock. Although they must have spoken some sort of Arabic dialect amongst themselves, they used as their official language Aramaic, the *lingua franca* of that period. Until recently all that was preserved of their written material were thousands of short rock inscriptions mainly above their tombs, all written in a lapidary, peculiar script. Now, suddenly, Babata's archive gave us for the first time several papyri written by the official Nabataean scribes, rich in content, terminology and philological data.

Towards the end of the first century AD – a couple of decades after the destruction of Jerusalem by Titus – Babata's father, Shimeon, settled in the village of Mahoza on the southern tip of the Dead Sea, within the boundaries of the district of the Biblical city of Zoar, which together with Sodom and Gomorrah formed part of the famous Dead Sea Pentapolis (it was in Zoar that Lot found refuge when Sodom and Gomorrah were destroyed).

Shimeon acquired from his Nabataean neighbours some plots of land, including palm-groves; the relevant Nabataean documents in our possession are deeds relating to the sale of those palm-groves, or rather title-deeds which were transferred to him at the time of the purchase. Eventually they came into the hands of Babata together with the other property she inherited.

The earliest of the documents is also the longest, eighty-one centimetres, containing ten lines on the *interior* (written in very cursive script) and forty-two on its *exterior* (written in a most elegant hand, obviously by a trained clerk). This deed was damaged by a moth, which – as seen in the picture – fortunately nibbled at the document mainly between the lines. . . .

The deed was written 'on the eighth of Elul [i.e. 10 September] in the twenty-third year of Rabael, the king, King of the Nabataeans who maintained life and brought deliverance to his people.' From the royal title it can be confidently assumed that the reference is to Rabael II (AD 70–106), the last Nabataean king, and therefore the date of the deed would be AD 93. The deed was drawn up in the district of Moab, which was part of the Nabataean kingdom. It deals with a bride-price and the consequent mortgaging of property of a certain 'Amat'isi (hand-maid of Isis) daughter of Kamanu son of 'Amru'ami, given to her by her husband Maqnamu son of 'Authillahi son of Halfillahi and vouched for by 'the guarantor 'Abd'amru'. This property, it seems, must have eventually been purchased by Shimeon.

Another 'tied deed', concerning a palm-grove, was written 'on the third of Kislev, in the twenty-eighth year of Rabael'. In addition the deed is dated 'in the lifetime of 'Obdath the son of Rabael the king, King of the Nabataeans who maintained life and brought deliverance to his people and [in the times] of Gamilath and Hagru his "sisters", queens of the Nabataeans, children of Maniku the king, King of the Nabataeans, the son of Haretath, King of the Nabataeans, who loved his people.' This document mentions the existence of a 'crown prince', ' 'Obdath the son of Rabael', who was not known from any other source.

The previous document dealt with a palm-grove, which according to the present document was acquired on 18 December AD 99. The palm-grove was indeed at a 'good address' to judge by one of its boundaries: 'To the south the grove of our lord Rabael the king.' This deed as well as many others – and similar to those from the Bar-Kokhba times already discussed – mentions a very important aspect of the property: its 'water rights': 'one hour every Sunday, every year, for ever', The document then proceeds to reassure the buyer and his heirs about all the rights concerning the grove, as well as their protection from appeals and claims of all kinds and against 'every man far or near'. Here the document is extremely rich in legal terms, some of which are identical with

An intelligent moth

A genealogy of the Nabataean kings

A palm-grove at a 'good address'

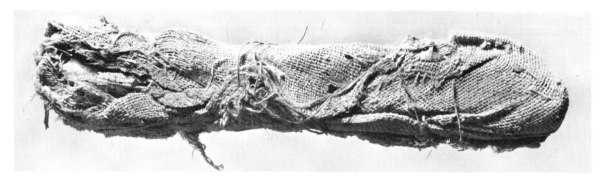

The 'gift deed' as it was found, well protected by wrapping

those found in the fifth century BC in Aramaic documents from Egypt, as well as in Jewish mediaeval legal documents – showing the strong tradition of legal phrasing.

This document was of extreme importance for the 'case' of Babata, and it was found very well protected by additional sack wrapping. It is, in fact, the first in a series of documents directly concerned with Babata and her immediate family. It is a 'tied deed', written in Aramaic along twenty-nine lines on the *interior* and forty-two lines on the *exterior*. Historically its chief value is in its being the only extant gift deed from Mishnaic times, in fact from the days of Rabbi Aqiba. As is well known, then as now, gifts of property made during the lifetime of the giver are extremely 'tricky' legal documents since their main purpose is usually the evasion of tax. Our document is also full of technical terms and data related to methods of land-registration. For Babata the importance of this document was in its clear definition of many of her pieces of property which she had inherited from her mother. The deed must have been drafted by a clever lawyer who was conversant with both Roman and Jewish law concerning 'gift deeds'. Shimeon managed by this document to get away with just about everything. The document is dated 'In the consulship of Lucius Catilius Severus for the second time and Marcus Aurelius Antoninus in the third year of Imperator Caesar Traianus Hadrianus Augustus and according to the era of this province [i.e. Provincia Arabia] on the twenty-fourth Tammuz year 15'; all that means 13 July AD 120. The deed was issued in 'the Mahoz of 'Agaltain' and the property referred to in it was situated in Mahoza which in the Greek deeds appears also as 'the village of Maoza.'

The deed begins with a clause stating that all the property listed in it is given by Shimeon as 'a gift in perpetuity' and continues: 'Of my own free will, I Shimeon son of Menahem, who live in Mahoza, give to you, Miriam, my wife daughter of Yehoseph son of Menashe, all that I possess in Mahoza.' The deed then goes on to list the various possessions which consist of houses, courtyards, gardens and groves, all precisely defined by their boundaries and 'water rights', as for example: 'Water – together with the heirs of Yehoseph son of Dormenes – one hour and half of three hours'; or: 'Water rights: Sunday, half an hour from the stream's water, together with the heirs of . . . and Monday half an hour . . .'; or again: 'Water rights, Wednesday one hour . . .'. Shimeon not only gives his wife all his property but also 'all that I shall purchase and that shall be mine henceforth'. Naturally enough Shimeon would not give away all he has or might have in the future without some conditions, and it is here particularly that the lawyer must have been of invaluable help for these are the conditions:

1. Shimeon reserves for himself the right of *usufruct*, possession, payment of debts and the right to live in the compounds and houses during his lifetime.

2. Miriam shall continue to perform all the duties of a wife as she has in the past and until the day of his death: 'that you shall be my wife as before and care for me out of the specified lots of this gift, until the day when I go to my last resting place.'

3. Here Shimeon wants to protect the future interests of both his wife and his daughter Babata: should their daughter, Babata, be widowed, she shall be entitled to live in one of the houses specified in the deed, but only until such time as she may remarry.

The deed is a mine of legal formulas designed to safeguard the recipient and her heirs from all possible claims. I must add that the deed permits Shimeon to sell, during his lifetime, some of his property, but only as may be required 'for my maintenance'. Thus we have a classical 'gift deed' which, although it was legally a binding, irrevocable document, still enabled the donor to incorporate in it any conditions he wanted.

Another well-guarded and specially wrapped document turned out to be Babata's *Kethuba* (marriage contract). This *Kethuba*, and two others somewhat less well preserved but of approximately the same period which were found in Wadi Murabba'at, are the only ones we have from the Mishnaic period and contain many interesting phrases. The date of our *Kethuba* is unfortunately damaged, so it would have been difficult to tell on the face of it if the *Kethuba* (marked on its back as: 'the *Kethuba* of Babata the daughter of Shimeon') pertained to her first or second marriage, were it not for the fact that the sum of money she was given by her husband was 'a hundred Tyrians', which according to Jewish law was the sum paid to a widow or a divorcee. So it must have been the *Kethuba* of her second marriage, to Yehudah son of Eleazar. This assumption is confirmed also by the fact that it is written in the handwriting of Yehudah as we know it from the other documents.

It is interesting that the opening formula declares that the marriage is performed according to 'the law of Moses and the Jews', and not as was the custom later and to this very day 'according to the law of Moses and Israel'. In fact some allusion in the

Babata's marriage contract

237

right Babata's marriage contract as it
was found in its wrapping and
(*far right*) after the removal of the
wrapping, showing further strings
tying the folded documents

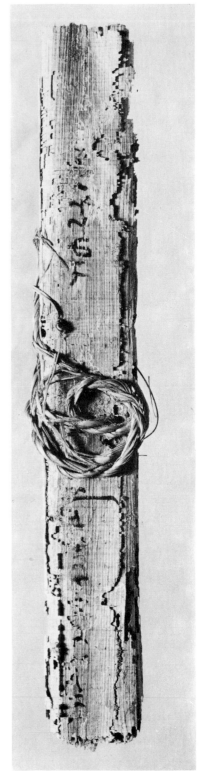

Mishna to pre-Bar-Kokhba *Kethuboth* indicates that this was in fact the formula (see, for example, the Palestinian Talmud, *Kethuboth* 4, 8 and the Mishna, *Kethuboth* VII: 6). We may therefore assume that the formula 'Moses and Israel' was introduced in Bar-Kokhba's times.

The second point of interest is that the *Kethuba* was written according to the practice of the region of Judaea (which comprised En-gedi) and not according to that prevailing in Jerusalem and Galilee. This is evident from the clause: 'If I go to my last resting place before you, you shall dwell in my house and receive maintenance from it and from my possessions, until such time as my heirs choose to pay you your *Kethuba* money.' This should be compared with what is stated in the Mishna, *Kethuboth* IV: 11–12: 'If he had not written for her "you shall dwell in my house and receive maintenance from my goods so long as you remain a widow in my house" he is still liable thereto, since this is a condition enjoined by the court. Thus used the people of Jerusalem to write; and the people of Galilee used to write after the same fashion as the people of Jerusalem. But the people of Judah used to write ". . . until such time as the heirs are minded to give you your *Kethuba*. . . ." '

On 6 May 124, there is still no indication of a union between Yehudah and Babata (which must have happened shortly afterwards), but this is the date of the document which first mentions Yehudah. It is an extraordinarily important Greek document, because of the light it sheds on En-gedi in the period just before the Bar-Kokhba Revolt and on the relations between the Roman soldiers and the local Jewish residents. The document is drawn up 'in En-gedi, village of the Lord Caesar'. En-gedi had always been considered 'crown property' because of its wealth in spices, particularly the famous balsam. In our earlier discussion of the letters and the deeds we mentioned that in Bar-Kokhba's time En-gedi became 'the property of the house of Israel', and the 'village of the Lord Caesar' that 'of the President of Israel'. Yehudah, in this deed, acknowledges that he borrowed the sum of sixty *denarii* of silver from Magonius Valens, a centurion of the *Cohors I miliaria Thracum*, i.e. a captain in a battalion of Thrace auxiliaries – obviously the commander of the Roman garrison in En-gedi. The loan was made against a mortgage on his father's (Eleazar son of Khthusion) house 'for which I have the authority of hypothecating and letting from the said Eleazaros'. The interest on the loan which Yehudah undertakes to pay is twelve per cent, or in the phrasing of the deed: 'I shall pay to you monthly the rate of one *denarius* in 100 *denarii*.'

Very little had been known about En-gedi of that period from previous archaeological exploration, and it is therefore of interest to learn about the neighbours of the aforesaid property: east – tents

Enter Yehudah son of Eleazar Khthusion

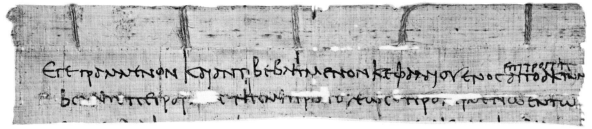

The top of the official extract from the acts of guardianship of the senate of Petra, dealing with Babata's orphan son

Babata and the orphan Yeshua

(probably the military camp); west – tents and the workshop of Eleazar; south – the *agora* (the public square) and Shimeon son of Matthaios; north – road and *praesidium* (military post). Thus we see that the Roman garrison was posted right in the heart of Engedi. One may assume that it was eliminated a few years later, at the time of the Bar-Kokhba Revolt, and as we have mentioned earlier, the Roman bronze vessels found in the Cave of Letters may have originally belonged to this garrison.

We have another interesting Greek document of the same year, which introduces to us one of the subjects most prominent in Babata's legal preoccupations: the guardians of her son by her deceased first husband. This document is an official extract from the acts of guardianship of the senate of 'Petra the metropolis'. The text runs: 'And of Iassouos the Jew son of Iassouos of the village of Maoza, Abdobdas Illoutha and Ioanes Eglas.' This extract would have been quite unintelligible, were it not for the following documents from which we know that 'Abd'obdath son of 'Illoutha (a Nabataean) and Yohanan Egla were the two appointed guardians of Yeshua son of Yeshua, the orphan, to whom we shall return in due course. There are two other points of interest in this unique document, which contribute to the history of Petra and the Province. It used to be an accepted view that in Hadrian's times Petra ceased to be the capital of the province and Bosra had been named instead, with the seat of the Roman governor moved to it. Our document and others from Babata's archive prove that this assumption was unfounded. The second point was the mention made of the Aphrodite temple, where the acts of guardianship were issued. This must have been an important building, and I believe it should be identified with the main temple of Petra, called by the Arabs 'the palace of the daughter of Pharaoh', which is Petra's commanding monument. Recent excavations at the site prove that contrary to previous thinking this temple was built before the times of Hadrian.

Babata takes the initiative

The problem of the guardians of the orphan now occupies the mind of Babata. In a document issued on 12 October 125, she summons Yohanan Egla to appear 'before the judgement seat of Julius Julianos the governor in Petra the metropolis of Arabia . . . until our case is heard'. The case is defined earlier in the document: 'since you did not give . . . to the said orphan . . . as Abdobdas

Illoutha has given'. (Through this and the following document, incidentally, we learn of the existence of a governor of Arabia, Julius Julianos, hitherto unknown.)

However, the main interest lies in the second document of the same date (12 October 125) which is an affidavit made by Babata, in court, against the two guardians. The affidavit is submitted on Babata's behalf through 'her guardian for the sake of this act, Yehudah, son of Khthusion, who being present, signed'. Yehudah here is not yet described as Babata's (second) husband, but possibly their relations were already quite intimate, and thus he served as her *epitropos*, as required by Roman law. Babata's application to the court is for cessation of the guardianship of her son, because of the guardians' failure to pay maintenance. She suggests a new arrangement, whereby the money held in trust by the guardians be turned over to her against adequate security, in exchange for which she offers to pay higher interest, or in her own words: 'give me the money against security, my property serving as hypothec, and I shall pay the interest of the money one and a half *denarii* [per month] in a hundred [as against one per hundred paid by the guardians] in order that thereby my son may be brilliantly [*sic!*] saved thanks to the most happy times of the governorship of Julius Julianos the governor into whose presence I Babata summoned you because of the refusal of Ioanes, the afore-written guardian, to pay the aliments.' It is interesting that at the bottom of the document, Yehudah testifies that he 'wrote on her behalf, having been asked, because she does not know how to write, and seven witnesses affixed their signatures to it'. There is an additional line at the bottom: 'He who wrote this is Theenas [Tehina] son of Simon, scribe.' On top of the above line there are subscriptions made in Aramaic, by Yehudah, who is defined as Babata's 'lord [i.e. guardian] in whose presence Babata testified as was written above'. Below his writing we find 'Abd'obdath's writing that all was written in the presence of himself and 'his colleague', Yohanan. Below that there is a short line in Aramaic: 'Yohanan son of Alex [Egla] in the hand of his son Yehoseph.' Obviously he too could not write!

The next document dated 2 December 127 is perhaps one of the most significant in Babata's archive. On that day, Babata, accompanied by Yehudah, who again serves as her 'lord', goes east of the Dead Sea to Rabbath-Moab (the capital of Moab) to declare her property before the Roman district commander, a certain Priscus, because 'a census of Arabia was being held by T. Aninius Sextius Florentinus', the governor of Arabia. Incidentally, the tomb of Florentinus was discovered in Petra a long time ago with an inscription listing all his titles, including the fact that he was governor of Provincia Arabia. The tomb was erected by his son. Some scholars suspected that Florentinus was governor of Arabia

'I swear by the Tyche of Lord Caesar'

241

right The 'guardians' deed before opening and (*far right*) the same deed with the *exterior* opened. The *interior* is still folded with its 'ties'. Note the subscriptions in Aramaic and Nabataean

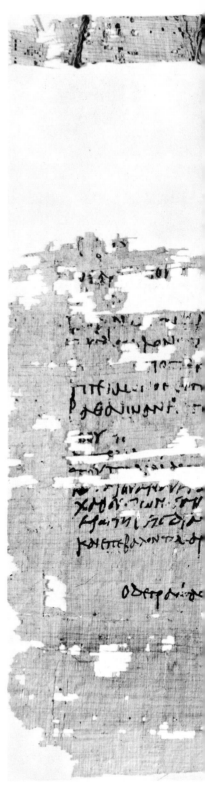

ΤΡΑΙΔΝΟΥΔΕ ΟΙ ΔΝ ΕΚΑΛΕΦΟΡΟΣ ... ΕΚΑΝΤΙ ...
ΝΟΥΣΤΡΑ ... ΛΝΤ

... ΤΩΝ ΕΛΟ ... ΓΑΛΩΝΟΣ ΤΟΥ ...
ΤΟΥ ΤΟ ΤΕΤ ΑΚΝΟΘΑ ... ΕΤ ... ΕΡΟΤΩΙΝ ...
... ΤΙΝΩΝ ... ΤΟΚΟΥ ... ΤΟΥ ...

... ΕΧΕ ΤΕΤΟ ΟΡΦΑΝΟΥ ΔΙΟ ΤΙ ... ΤΡΟΠΟΙΗ ... ΙΝ ...
... ΠΟΘΙΚΝ ΤΩΝ ΝΙ ... ΧΟΝ ΤΩΝ ΝΟΥ ...
... ΕΚ ... ΒΙΝ ... ΝΗΦΟΡΙΝ ... ΚΝΣΤΟΘΕΙ ... ΔΙΟ ...
... ΤΟΙΣ ΚΝ ... ΓΑΛΩΝΕ ...
... ΤΡΟΦΩΝ ... ΕΡ ...
... ΤΟΥ ΟΡΦΑΝΟΥ ΔΕ ΛΗΓΕ ΤΟ ...
... ΓΕ ΔΙΚΝ ΩΝ Α ΚΕΡΔΟΝ ΥΠ ΤΥΡΙΟΝ ΤΟΥ ΟΡΦΑΝΟΥ Σ ΔΙΔΟΝ ...
ΤΡΟΠΟΙ ... ΤΟΙ ΒΒΑΟΔ ... ΤΡΟ ΕΡΟΤΟ ... ΤΡΟΣ ...
... ΩΝΟΣ ...
... ΝΟΟ ...
...
... ΓΑΛΩΝΟΝ ΚΝΟΡΙ ...

during the reign of Hadrian, but his precise years of governorship were unknown. Now we know them: 127–9. In 125 the governor was still Julius Julianos (see above) and in 130 it was already Haterius Nepos (see below). Babata is introduced in the document as 'Babata [daughter of] Shimeon of Maoza in the sub-district of Zoar, in the district of Petra, living in her own premises in the said Maoza', and then: 'I declare what I possess there, in the presence of my guardian, Yehudah [son of] Eleazar of the village of En-gedi in the district of Jericho in [the province of] Judaea, living in his own premises in the said Maoza.'

We learn interesting details about the administrative arrangements in Judaea (which until the Bar-Kokhba Revolt was an independent province of that name, but afterwards became Syria-Palaestina, to be known later by the Arabs as Falastin and otherwise as Palestine), and the status of En-gedi, which at that time was part of the district of Jericho.

The tomb of Sextius Florentinus, Governor of the Provincia Arabia, at Petra. Florentinus is mentioned in a dated document in Babata's archive

244

This being an official declaration for the purpose of the census, i.e. taxes, Babata took particular care to define her property with great precision as to names of groves, area boundaries and particularly the exact crops of dates, according to their varieties. Some of the groves are familiar from the gift deed of her father, mentioned above. It seems to me – knowing her property as I do from other documents – that Babata may have declared less than she actually had. If this is indeed so, I hope she may be forgiven, seeing that at the end of the document there appears a translation of the oath she had taken: 'I swear by the Tyche of the Lord Caesar to have declared *bona fide* as written above.'

On 2 February 127 there is a formal agreement – in Greek and Aramaic – between Babata and Yehudah, in which she is now formally called 'his wife'. Subject: Yehudah acknowledges receiving from Babata a deposit (*paratheke*) of 300 silver *denarii*. He undertakes to give these back to her 'whenever she desires'. Should he

A loan?

A drawing of the tomb of Sextius Florentinus

refuse, he would be liable according to 'the law of deposits' to repay her double the amount and damages. Moreover, in case of non-compliance, Babata or 'whoever may bring forward this agreement on her behalf' will get its value 'from his property . . . which he possesses and which he may acquire in addition'. In view of the common practice prevalent in the Roman Empire, this agreement may be suspected of being a disguised marriage-gift. The fact that Babata still possessed this document after Yehudah's death, must have been the basis for her claim to his property, partially contested by his relatives.

Enter Shelamzion

At this stage we become acquainted with a new member of the family of Babata's second husband, his daughter by his other marriage: Shelamzion. She played an important role in Babata's subsequent litigations. A Greek document dated 5 April 128 is in fact the marriage contract of Shelamzion to a certain Yehudah Kimber, son of Hananiah, a native of En-gedi. This contract, like the normal *Kethuba*, was of the utmost importance to the wife, and it was found well wrapped in a piece of cloth. It is interesting because it illustrates some traits of assimilation among the wealthy Jewish families of the time, not only in the fact that it was drawn up in Greek, but also because it specifically says that it is written according to 'Hellenic law'. In this document Yehudah son of Eleazar, alias Khthusion, 'gave into marriage his own daughter Shelamzion [in the Greek: Selampsione], virgin, to Yehudah, nicknamed Kimber, son of Hananiah [son of] Somala, both from the village of En-gedi in Judaea, dwelling here' (i.e. in Mahoza). Shelamzion brings to her husband 'according to the law', on account of dowry, feminine adornment consisting of silver and gold and clothing, evaluated by common consent as both acknowledge, as equivalent to two hundred silver *denarii*. Yehudah Kimber acknowledges further that he actually received the above dowry 'by hand on the spot from Yehudah her father', and he undertakes 'to owe it to the said Shelamzion his wife, together with another three hundred *denarii*'. The importance of this to Babata was in the fact that Kimber gave as securities for his obligations 'all the property which he owns in his said village [i.e. En-gedi] as well as here, and which he might acquire'. This undertaking is valid 'in any manner that his wife Shelamzion may choose, or whosoever acting through her or on her behalf may choose'. After that, there are subscriptions in Aramaic in which the father reaffirms that he gave his virgin daughter Shelamzion to Kimber as written above, and Kimber acknowledges, in fairly good handwriting, that he owes his wife Shelamzion the sum mentioned above.

How this document made its way into the hands of Babata, we can only guess. After the death of Shelamzion's father, Babata must have been entrusted with her step-daughter's affairs, which

included property in both Mahoza and En-gedi. Furthermore in the next document (16 April 128), barely eleven days after Shelamzion's marriage, Yehudah Khthusion, her father, gives her as an inheritance after his death, half of some property in En-gedi which must have belonged to other members of his family, or so they claimed.

Inheritance problems

Soon afterwards, Babata became a widow for the second time. Yehudah her husband must have died not later than 11 September AD 130 and most probably before 19 June of that year. By then we have some documents showing that Babata, after the death of her husband, became the owner of several palm-groves which had belonged to him. She sold crops of dates from the said groves and the buyer acknowledged the deal by referring to the crops 'of the groves of Yehudah Khthusion your deceased husband, in Maoza'. The list of palm-groves is not the same as the ones she declared in the census, which were her's through her father, and the document states quite plainly the basis of Babata's ownership of her husband's groves: 'which you hold [says the buyer of the crops] as you say in lieu of your bride-money and due'. Now the purpose of the IOU which we mentioned earlier becomes clear. From now on Babata, burdened with additional property, begins a long engagement in litigation with certain members of her deceased husband's family. Her troubles come from two unexpected quarters.

The mysterious Julia Crispina

The death of the wealthy Yehudah, who owned property in both En-gedi and Mahoza, demanded the division of his belongings, since some of his property belonged to Babata, some to his daughter and some to other members of his family. A document dated 19 June 130 cedes to Shelamzion 'out of the property of Eleazar, also called Khthusion, son of Yehudah, your grandfather, a compound with all its rights in En-gedi and all the houses in it'. The cession is made on behalf 'of the orphans of Yeshua son of Eleazar Khthusion' (i.e. the children of Shelamzion's deceased uncle), by their guardian 'Besas son of Yeshua from En-gedi who lives now in Mazra'a'. (Incidentally this is the first known mention of a village by that name, still preserved today in that very form in the name of an Arab village in the 'tongue' of the Dead Sea, due east of Masada.) Besas appears with some mysterious Roman woman,

The two deeds dealing with Shelamzion's property wrapped together

by the name of Julia Crispina, who is described as *episkopos*, but the documents shed no light on the nature of her 'overseership'. She appears later, in lieu of Besas who is indisposed, in a legal dispute with Babata. Professor Polotsky when studying these documents discovered an interesting allusion to a woman of the same name in a document from the Fayyum in Egypt, dated 24 July 133, in which she declares her property there. 'It would be a strange coincidence indeed', writes Professor Polotsky, 'if two women of the same Roman name had been living at about the same time in the same area. The dates would seem to suggest that after the spread of the Jewish Revolt Julia Crispina broke off her Jewish connections and transferred her activities to Egypt, if indeed they had not extended to Egypt even before.'

The settlement between Shelamzion and her orphan nephews must have been a relatively easy matter. The real trouble, as far as Babata was concerned, began when Besas and Julia, on behalf of the orphans, sued her concerning a palm-grove in Mahoza which they claimed had belonged to the orphans. This must have been a very important case for Babata, since several of her documents are related to it.

Summons, summons . . .

A document dated 17 November 130 is a summons to Babata, written by a clerk named Germanos (son of) Judas (!): 'In the presence of the undersigned witnesses, Besas [son of] Yeshua, guardian of the orphans of Yeshua [son of] Eleazar Khthusion, called upon Babata [daughter of] Shimeon of Maoza, to come with him to Haterius Nepos, the governor [*legatus* and *propraetor*], to Petra or elsewhere in his province, on account of a palm-grove belonging to the said orphans, which you hold in your possession by force.' (Incidentally, again we learn from this document the name of yet another hitherto unknown governor of the province.) This law-suit was a protracted one, and from July AD 131 we have another, most interesting document – a summons once more – which is unfortunately not very well preserved. In it Julia Crispina summons Babata 'whereas Besas [son of] Yeshua the guardian of the said orphans, is ill and was unable to summon'. There follows a repetition of the accusation. However, Babata 'kicks back' through a Nabataean lawyer, or guardian, who resides near the court at

Petra: 'To this replied Babata [daughter of] Shimeon through her guardian Maras Abdalgou of Petra, saying: "Since earlier you summoned me . . . using violence against me and defaming me, I wrote a complaint against you to His Excellency the Governor which he acknowledged. . . . And now I summon you. . . ." '
Petra is called in this document 'Hadriane Petra' – in honour of Hadrian's visit there – which proves the validity of the assumption of some scholars that his visit to Petra was in AD 131. We know now that the visit was rather early in that year: our papyrus is the earliest reference to Hadrian's Petra in documents.

Of all the litigation and court summonses, the one which must have really infuriated Babata concerned her second husband's other wife, Miriam, who resided in En-gedi. The following summons, dated 7 July 131, is rather amusing, were it not tragic for those concerned: 'In the presence of the witnesses . . . Babata [daughter of] Shimeon of Maoza summoned Miriam [Mariame] daughter of Be'ayan of En-gedi to come forth together with her to Haterius Nepos the governor wherever he may be present; since you [Miriam] plundered everything in the house of Yehudah son of Eleazar Khthusion my and your husband. . . .'

The other wife

The case was obviously not so simple, as the document demonstrates: 'To this replied Miriam, saying: "I warned you before not to approach the property of my husband . . . you have no claim against the said Yehudah my husband regarding the property." ' Was Haterius Nepos endowed with the wisdom of Solomon? That we do not know.

This document, however, explains how Babata eventually, when the revolt broke out, found her way to En-gedi; not solely because of her property there, or because of her own numerous relatives in that place, but because through her second husband's other wife (Miriam, daughter of Be'ayan), she found herself remotely connected to the commander of En-gedi in Bar-Kokhba's administration: Yehonathan son of Be'ayan, the addressee of the Bar-Kokhba letters, Miriam's brother.

The last 'entry' in Babata's archive again concerns her son by her first husband, whom she calls 'Yeshua son of Yeshua my orphan son'. Apparently her previous petition failed since the son is not her ward. Instead he is under the guardianship of Shimeon 'the hunchback' son of Yohanan son of Egla, i.e. the son of the unsatisfactory guardian appointed in AD 124. The document is actually a receipt, in which Babata confirms – in Greek as well as in Aramaic (with a Greek translation of the Aramaic) – the receipt 'from you on account of aliments and clothing of the said Yeshua my son, six *denarii* of silver from the first of the month of *Panemos* [June] of the said 27th year [of Provincia Arabia] until the thirtieth of *Gorpiaios* [August] three full months'. Her 'guardian' for this act is a certain Babeli son of Menahem of Mahoza. Was he just a

The last document

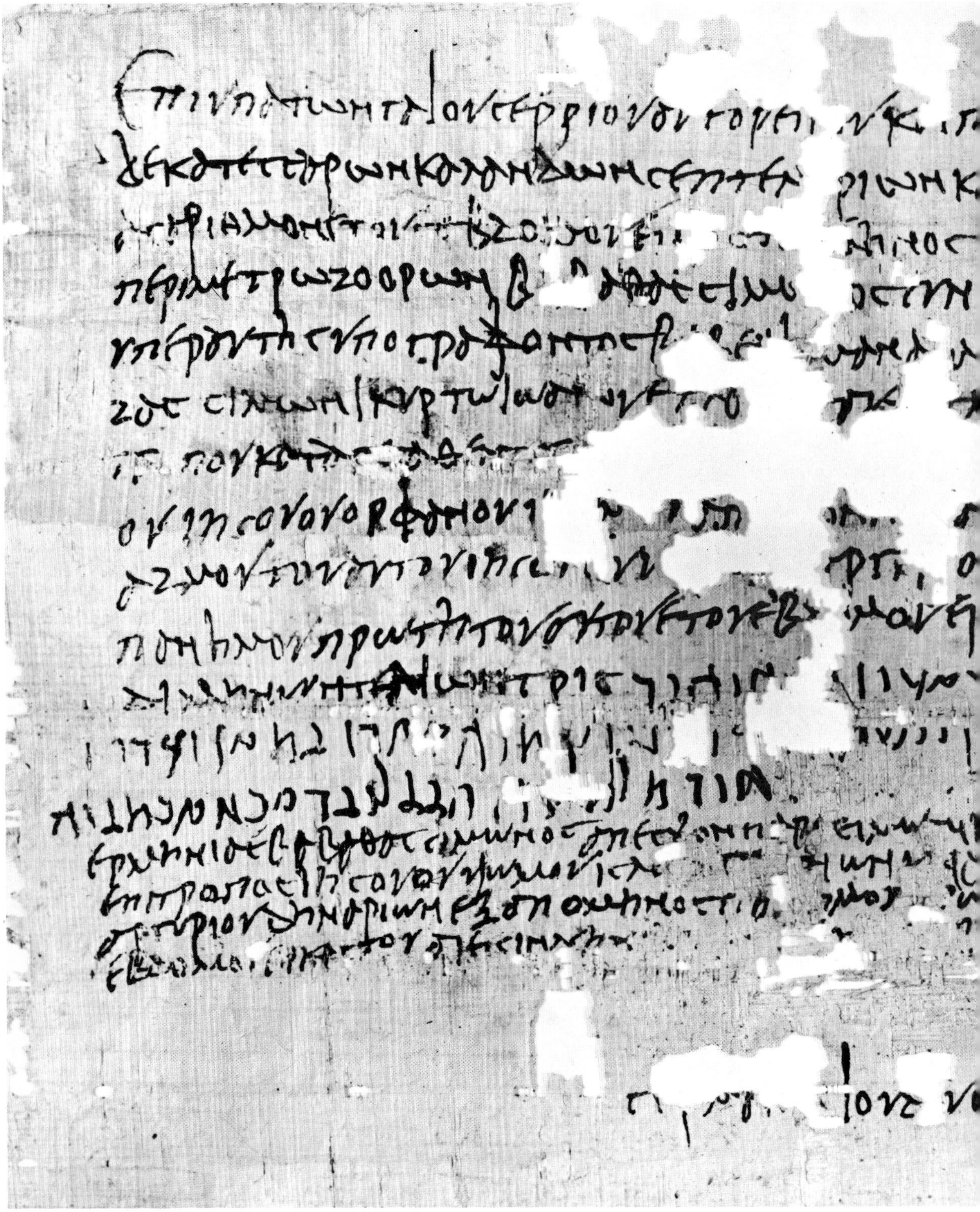

The latest deed in Babata's archive dated 19 August AD 132.
Note the subscriptions in Aramaic

The bivouacs of team D near the remains of the Roman camp

'guardian' or is our formidable Babata married for the third time?

The last document is dated 19 August AD 132, and this is hardly accidental. It was precisely in that year that the war of Bar-Kokhba began. Was Babata forced to flee from the Provincia Arabia to En-gedi? Or was she a 'Zionist' who migrated to the newly-established Jewish State? This we shall never know.

'*They were sitting in a cave and they heard a noise from above the cave and they thought that the enemies had come upon them*' (Babylonian Talmud, Shabbath 60a).

The end

What befell Babata and her compatriots from En-gedi until they met their death in the Cave of Letters, we may never find out. But we can guess. When Babata arrived in En-gedi, Bar-Kokhba was already proclaimed President of Israel. Yehonathan, son of Be'ayan, and Masabala assumed the command and administration of En-gedi on behalf of Bar-Kokhba. The 'crown property' had reverted to the 'President of Israel' from 'the Lord Caesar'. New lease documents were promulgated in Hebrew, on behalf of Bar-Kokhba, proudly bearing the dates according to 'Shimeon son of Kosiba, President of Israel', instead of the hated dating by the consuls, the imperator, and the era of the Provincia.

However, the gathering storm unleashed thunder and lightning. Hadrian mobilised his entire force and put it under the command of his best general, Julius Severus. Bar-Kokhba, in retreat, found himself short of men and food. He sent desperate despatches to the oasis of En-gedi – for a while still remote from the battle-field – requesting provisions and the mobilisation of fugitives, but apparently in vain. The turn of the son of Be'ayan, Masabala and their men, was to come soon. The Romans approached En-gedi. The people of En-gedi, with their families and whatever possessions they could carry with them, fled to the caves in surrounding canyons, well-prepared and stocked in advance. Yehonathan ben Be'ayan and his entourage (including Babata) took refuge in the biggest cave of all, the Cave of Letters. But the Romans discovered their hiding place soon enough and posted garrisons above the caves. . . .

Archaeologists are also human beings, and as human beings, they are often emotionally attached to the history of their own people.

Descending daily over the precipice, crossing the dangerous ledge to the caves, working all day long in the stench of the bats, confronted from time to time with the tragic remains of those besieged and trapped – we found that our emotions were a mixture of tension and awe, yet astonishment and pride at being part of the reborn State of Israel after a Diaspora of 1,800 years. Here were we, living in tents erected by the Israel Defence Forces, walking every day through the ruins of a Roman camp which caused the death of our forefathers. Nothing remains here today of the Romans save a heap of stones on the face of the desert, but here the descendants of the besieged were returning to salvage their ancestors' precious belongings.

Appendix of references to Bar-Kokhba

Selected Ancient Sources
For short, additional references, see Chapter 1

JEWISH SOURCES

Some extracts from the Talmud and the Midrash
There are several parallels to the following
passages in the Palestinian Talmud (mainly
Ta'anith 68–9) and other Midrashim, with minor
variants. For convenience's sake, the extracts
were taken from two sources:
a) The Babylonian Talmud, Gittin 57–8.
Translation by M. Simon under the Editorship of
Isidore Epstein, The Soncino Press, London, 1936.
b) Midrash Rabbah, Lamentations.
Translation by A. Cohen under the Editorship of
H. Freedman and M. Simon, The Soncino Press,
London, 1939, pp. 157–61.

Bar-Kokhba and Rabbi Aqiba

When R. Akiba [Aqiba] beheld Bar Koziba he exclaimed, 'This is the king Messiah!' R. Johanan b.
Tortha retorted: 'Akiba, grass will grow in your
cheeks[1] and he will still not have come!'
(*Mid. Lam.*)

1 or: jawbones

Bar-Kokhba's courage and might

Eighty thousand trumpeters besieged Bethar where
Bar Koziba was located who had with him two
hundred thousand men with an amputated finger.
The Sages sent him the message, 'How long will you
continue to make the men of Israel blemished?' He
asked them, 'How else shall they be tested?' They
answered, 'Let anyone who cannot uproot a cedar
from Lebanon be refused enrolment in your army.'
He thereupon had two hundred thousand men of
each class; and when they went forth to battle they
cried, '[O God,] neither help us nor discourage[1] us!'
That is what is written, *Hast not Thou, O God, cast us
off? And go not forth, O God, with our hosts* (Psalms
60:12). And what used Bar Koziba to do? He would
catch the missiles from the enemy's catapults on one
of his knees and hurl them back, killing many of the
foe. On that account R. Akiba made his remark.[2]
(*Mid. Lam.*)

1 or: disgrace   2 as above

Bar-Kokhba, Rabbi Eleazar of Modi'in and Hadrian

For three and a half years the Emperor Hadrian
surrounded Bethar.[1] In the city was R. Eleazar of
Modim[2] who continually wore sackcloth and fasted,
and he used to pray daily, 'Lord of the Universe, sit
not in judgment today!' so that [Hadrian] thought of
returning home. A Cuthean[3] went and found him
and said, 'My lord, so long as that old cock wallows
in ashes you will not conquer the city. But wait for
me, because I will do something which will enable
you to subdue it to-day.' He immediately entered the
gate of the city, where he found R. Eleazar standing
and praying. He pretended to whisper in the ear of
R. Eleazar of Modim. People went and informed Bar
Koziba, 'Your friend, R. Eleazar, wishes to surrender
the city to Hadrian.' He sent and had the Cuthean
brought to him and asked, 'What did you say to
him?' He replied, 'If I tell you, the king will kill me;
and if I do not tell you, you will kill me. It is better
that I should kill myself and the secrets of the government be not divulged.' Bar Koziba was convinced
that R. Eleazar wanted to surrender the city, so when
the latter finished his praying he had him brought
into his presence and asked him, 'What did the
Cuthean tell you?' He answered, 'I do not know
what he whispered in my ear, nor did I hear anything, because I was standing in prayer and am unaware what he said.' Bar Koziba flew into a rage,
kicked him with his foot and killed him. A *Bath Kol*[4]
issued forth and proclaimed, '*Woe to the worthless
shepherd that leaveth the flock! The sword shall be upon
his arm, and upon his right eye*' (Zech. 11:17). It inti-
mated to him, 'Thou hast paralysed the arm of Israel
and blinded their right eye; therefore shall thy arm
wither and thy right eye grow dim!' Forthwith the
sins [of the people] caused Bethar to be captured. Bar
Koziba was slain and his head taken to Hadrian. 'Who
killed him?' asked Hadrian. A Cuthean said to him,
'I killed him.' 'Bring his body to me,' he ordered. He
went and found a snake encircling its neck; so [Had-
rian when told of this] exclaimed, 'If his God had not
slain him who could have overcome him?' And there
was applied to him the verse, *Except their Rock had
given them over* (Deuteronomy 32:30).
(*Mid. Lam.*)

1 most probably the duration of the whole war
2 the birth-place of the Maccabees
3 Samaritan
4 a heavenly voice

A similar story about the two brothers

There were two brothers in Kefar Haruba[1] who did not allow any Roman to pass there but they killed him. They said, 'The conclusion of the whole matter is that we must take Hadrian's crown and set it upon our own head.' They heard that the Romans were coming towards them; and when they set out against them an old man met them and said, 'May the Creator be your help against them!' They retorted, 'Let Him neither help us nor discourage[2] us!' Their sins immediately caused them to be slain [in the battle]. Their heads were brought to Hadrian, who asked, 'Who killed them?' A Cuthean replied, 'I slew them'; and the king ordered him to fetch their bodies. He went and found a snake encircling their necks; so [Hadrian when told of this] exclaimed, 'If their God had not slain them who could have overcome them?' And there was applied to them the verse, *Except their Rock had given them over* (Deuteronomy 32: 30).
(*Mid. Lam.*)

1 location unknown; perhaps in the vicinity of Qiryath Aravaya?
2 or: disgrace

Another cause for the fall of Bethar

'Through the shaft of a litter[1] Bethar was destroyed.' It was the custom when a boy was born to plant a cedar tree and when a girl was born to plant a pine tree, and when they married, the tree was cut down and a canopy made of the branches. One day the daughter of the Emperor was passing when the shaft of her litter broke, so they lopped some branches off a cedar tree and brought it to her. The Jews thereupon fell upon them and beat them. They reported to the Emperor that the Jews were rebelling, and he marched against them.
(*Gittin*).

1 or: a carriage axle

ROMAN ATROCITIES

The Genocide

R. Johanan said: *The voice is the voice of Jacob* (Genesis 27: 22) – the voice [of distress caused by] the Emperor Hadrian, who slew eighty thousand myriads of human beings at Bethar.
(*Mid. Lam.*)

They slew the inhabitants until the horses waded in blood up to the nostrils, and the blood rolled along stones of the size of forty *se'ah*[1] and flowed into the sea [staining it for] a distance of four miles. Should you say that [Bethar] is close to the sea; was it not in fact four miles[2] distant from it? Now Hadrian possessed a large vineyard[3] eighteen miles square, as far as from Tiberias to Sepphoris, and they surrounded it with a fence consisting of the slain at Bethar. Nor was it decreed that they should be buried until a certain king arose and ordered their interment. R. Huna said: On the day when the slain of Bethar were allowed burial, the benediction 'Who art kind and dealest kindly' was instituted – 'Who art kind' because the bodies did not putrefy, 'and dealest kindly' because they were allowed burial.[4]
(*Mid. Lam.*)

1 a measure
2 another version: forty miles
3 or: *circumvallatio*
4 Palestinian Talmud, Berakhoth 3d

He hath cut off in fierce anger all the horn of Israel (Lamentations 2: 3). R. Zera said in the name of R. Abbahu who quoted R. Johanan: These are the eighty [thousand] battle trumpets which assembled in the city of Bethar when it was taken and men, women and children were slain in it until their blood ran into the great sea. Do you think this was near? It was a whole *mile*[1] away. It has been taught: R. Eleazar the Great said: There are two streams in the valley of Yadaim,[2] one running in one direction and one in another, and the Sages estimated that [at that time] they ran with two parts water to one of blood. In a Baraitha it has been taught: For seven years the gentiles fertilised their vineyards with the blood of Israel without using manure.
(*Gittin*)

1 other version: four miles
2 locality unknown

The extermination of the children

R. Johanan said: The brains of three hundred children [were dashed] upon one stone, and three hundred baskets of capsules of phylacteries were found in Bethar, each basket being of the capacity of three *se'ah*,[1] so that there was a total of three hundred *se'ah*. R. Gamaliel said: There were five hundred schools in Bethar, and the smallest of them had not less than three hundred children. They used to say, 'If the enemy comes against us, with these styluses we will go out and stab them!' When, however, [the people's] sins did cause the enemy to come, they enwrapped each pupil in his book and burnt him, so that I alone was left. He applied to himself the verse, *Mine eye affecteth my soul, because of all the daughters* [i.e. inhabi-

tants] *of my city* (Lamentations 3 : 51).
(*Mid. Lam.*)

1 a measure

Rab Judah reported Samuel as saying in the name of Rabban Simeon b. Gamaliel: What is signified by the verse, *Mine eye affecteth my soul, because of all the daughters of my city* (Lamentations 3 :51). There were four hundred synagogues in the city of Bethar, and in every one were four hundred teachers of children, and each one had under him four hundred pupils, and when the enemy entered there they pierced them with their staves, and when the enemy prevailed and captured them, they wrapped them in their scrolls and burnt them with fire.
(*Gittin*)

Again the genocide

Rabbah Bar Hanah said in the name of R. Johanan: Forty se'ahs[1] of phylactery boxes[2] were found on the heads of the victims of Bethar. R. Jannai son of R. Ishmael said there were three chests each containing forty se'ahs.
(*Gittin*)

1 a measure
2 or: capsules

The voice is the voice of Jacob and the hands are the hands of Esau (Genesis 27: 22): 'the voice' here refers to [the cry caused by] the Emperor Hadrian who killed in Alexandria of Egypt sixty myriads on sixty myriads, twice as many as went forth from Egypt. '*The voice of Jacob*': this is the cry caused by the Emperor Vespasian[1] who killed in the city of Bethar four hundred thousand myriads, or as some say, four thousand myriads.
(*Gittin*)

1 a mistake for Hadrian

NON-JEWISH SOURCES
Dio Cassius (*Second - Third Centuries* AD)

At Jerusalem he[1] founded a city in place of the one which had been razed to the ground, naming it Aelia Capitolina, and on the site of the temple of the god[2] he raised a new temple to Jupiter. This brought on a war of no slight importance nor of brief duration, for the Jews deemed it intolerable that foreign races should be settled in their city and foreign religious rites planted there. So long, indeed, as Hadrian was close by in Egypt and again in Syria, they remained

quiet, save in so far as they purposely made of poor quality such weapons as they were called upon to furnish, in order that the Romans might reject them and they themselves might thus have the use of them; but when he went farther away, they openly revolted. To be sure, they did not dare try conclusions with the Romans in the open field, but they occupied the advantageous positions in the country and strengthened them with mines and walls, in order that they might have places of refuge whenever they should be hard pressed, and might meet together unobserved under ground; and they pierced these subterranean passages from above at intervals to let in air and light.

At first the Romans took no account of them. Soon, however, all Judaea had been stirred up, and the Jews everywhere were showing signs of disturbance, were gathering together, and giving evidence of great hostility to the Romans, partly by secret and partly by overt acts; many outside nations, too, were joining them through eagerness for gain, and the whole earth, one might almost say, was being stirred up over the matter. Then, indeed, Hadrian sent against them his best generals. First of these was Julius Severus, who was dispatched from Britain, where he was governor, against the Jews. Severus did not venture to attack his opponents in the open at any one point, in view of their numbers and their desperation, but by intercepting small groups, thanks to the number of his soldiers and his under-officers, and by depriving them of food and shutting them up, he was able, rather slowly, to be sure, but with comparatively little danger, to crush, exhaust and exterminate them. Very few of them in fact survived. Fifty of their most important outposts and nine hundred and eighty-five of their most famous villages were razed to the ground. Five hundred and eighty thousand men were slain in the various raids and battles, and the number of those that perished by famine, disease and fire was past finding out. Thus nearly the whole of Judaea was made desolate, a result of which the people had had forewarning before the war. For the tomb of Solomon, which the Jews regard as an object of veneration, fell to pieces of itself and collapsed, and many wolves and hyenas rushed howling into their cities. Many Romans, moreover, perished in this war. Therefore Hadrian in writing to the senate did not employ the opening phrase commonly affected by the emperors, 'If you and your children are in health, it is well; I and the legions are in health.'
(*Roman History, LXIX, 12–14. Translation by E. Cary, The Loeb Classical Library, Heinemann Ltd., London and Harvard University Press, 1925, Vol. VIII, pp. 447–51*)

1 Hadrian   2 i.e. the Jewish Temple

Justin (*Contemporary of Bar-Kokhba*)

The same writer[1] mentions the war of that time against the Jews and makes this observation, 'For in the present Jewish war it was only Christians whom Bar Chocheba, the leader of the rebellion of the Jews, commanded to be punished severely, if they did not deny Jesus as the Messiah and blaspheme him.'

(*Quoted by Eusebius in* Ecclesiastical History, *IV, 8. Translation by K. Lake, The Loeb Classical Library, Heinemann Ltd, London and Harvard University Press, 1926, pp. 322–3*)

1 Justin

Eusebius (*Third–Fourth Centuries* AD)

The rebellion of the Jews once more progressed in character and extent, and Rufus, the governor of Judaea, when military aid had been sent him by the Emperor, moved out against them, treating their madness without mercy. He destroyed in heaps thousands of men, women and children, and, under the law of war, enslaved their land. The Jews were at that time led by a certain Bar Chochebas,[1] which means 'star', a man who was murderous and a bandit, but relied on his name, as if dealing with slaves, and claimed to be a luminary who had come down to them from heaven and was magically enlightening those who were in misery. The war reached its height in the eighteenth year of the reign of Hadrian in Beththera,[2] which was a strong citadel not very far from Jerusalem; the siege lasted a long time before the rebels were driven to final destruction by famine and thirst and the instigator of their madness paid the penalty he deserved. Hadrian then commanded that by a legal decree and ordinances the whole nation should be absolutely prevented from entering from thenceforth even the district round Jerusalem, so that not even from a distance could it see its ancestral home. Ariston of Pella tells the story.[3] 'Thus when the city came to be bereft of the nation of the Jews, and its ancient inhabitants had completely perished, it was colonized by foreigners, and the Roman city which afterwards arose changed its name, and in honour of the reigning emperor Aelius Hadrian was called Aelia. The church, too, in it was composed of Gentiles, and after the Jewish bishops the first who was appointed to minister to those there was Marcus.

(Ecclesiastical History, *IV, 6. Translation by K. Lake, The Loeb Classical Library, Heinemann Ltd., London and Harvard University Press, 1926, Vol. I, pp. 311–13*)

1 literally: Son of the Star
2 Bethar
3 the book is not extant

Eusebius (*Third–Fourth Centuries* AD)

Hadrian's Year 16 (AD *132*) The Jews, who took up arms, devastated Palestine during the period in which the governor of the province was Tineus Rufus, to whom Hadrian sent an army in order to crush the rebels.

Hadrian's Year 17 (AD *133*) Cochebas, duke of the Jewish sect, killed the Christians with all kinds of persecutions, (when) they refused to help him against the Roman troops.

Hadrian's Year 18 (AD *134*), *Armenian Version: Year 19; AD 135*) The Jewish War that was conducted in Palestine reached its conclusion, all Jewish problems having been completely suppressed. From that time (on), the permission was denied them even to enter Jerusalem; first and foremost because of the commandment of God, as the prophets had prophesied; and secondly by authority of the interdictions of the Romans.

In Jerusalem the first bishop was appointed from among the gentiles, since bishops ceased to be appointed from among the Jews.

Hadrian's Year 20 (AD *136*) Aelia was founded by Aelius Hadrianus; and before its gate, that of the road by which we go to Bethlehem, he set up an idol of a pig in marble, signifying the subjugation of the Jews to Roman authority.

(*According to the Latin version of his Chronicle. Other short passages in Eusebius,* Demonstratio Evangelica, *which contain practically no further new data, are not quoted*)

Jerome (*Fourth–Fifth Centuries* AD)

. . . just as that famed Bar Chochabas, the instigator of the Jewish uprising, kept fanning a lighted blade of straw in his mouth with puffs of breath so as to give the impression that he was spewing out flames . . .

('*The Apology Against the Books of Rufinus' in Saint Jerome; Dogmatic and Polemical Works, translated by J. N. Hritzu in The Fathers of the Church, Vol. 53, Washington D. C., p. 202*)

Some extracts from the Commentary on the Old and New Testaments:

a) *On Isaiah 2: 15*
And those who ascribe this to the time of Vespasianus and Hadrian say that the writing here was completely fulfilled, for no high tower, no most fortified wall, no mightiest navy and not the most diligent in commerce – could overcome the might of the Roman Army; and the citizens of Judaea came to such distress that they, together with their wives, their children,

their gold and their silver, in which they trusted, *remained in underground tunnels and deepest caves* [author's italics]

b) *On Matthew 24: 15*

. . . or to the statue of the mounted Hadrian, which stands to this very day on the site of the Holy of Holies.

Epiphanius (*Fourth Century* AD)

And he went up to Jerusalem, the famous and illustrious city which Titus, the son of Vespasian, overthrew in the second year of his reign. And he found the temple of God trodden down and the whole city devastated save for a few houses and the church of God, which was small, where the disciples, when they had returned after the Saviour had ascended from the Mount of Olives, went to the upper room. For there it had been built, that is, in that portion of Zion which escaped destruction, together with blocks of houses in the neighbourhood of Zion and the seven synagogues which alone remained standing in Zion, like solitary huts, one of which remained until the time of Maximona the bishop and Constantine the king, 'like a booth in a vineyard,'[1] as it is written. Therefore Hadrian made up his mind to [re]build the city, but not the temple. And he took the Aquila mentioned above, who was a Greek interpreter.[2] Now Aquila was related to the king by marriage and was from Sinope in Pontus – and he established him there in Jerusalem as overseer of the work of building the city. And he gave to the city that was being built his own name and the appellation of the royal title. For as he was named Aelius Hadrian, so he also named the city Aelia.

15. So Aquila, while he was in Jerusalem, also saw the disciples of the disciples of the apostles flourishing in the faith and working great signs, healings and other miracles. For they were such as had come back from the city of Pella[3] to Jerusalem . . . they wrought great signs, as I have already said. So Aquila, after he had been strongly stirred in mind, believed in Christianity, and after a while, when he asked, he received the seal in Christ. But according to his former habit, while yet thinking the things of the heathen, he had been thoroughly trained in vain astronomy, so that also after he became a Christian he never departed from this fault of his, but every day he made calculations on the horoscope of his birth. He was reproved by the teachers, and they rebuked him for this every day but did not accomplish anything. But instead of standing rebuked, he became bold in disputation and

tried to establish things that have no existence, tales about fate. Hence, as one who proved useless and could not be saved, he was expelled from the church. But as one who had become embittered in mind over how he had suffered dishonour, he was puffed up with vain jealousy, and having cursed Christianity and renounced his life he became a proselyte and was circumcised as a Jew. And, being painfully ambitious, he dedicated himself to learning the language of the Hebrews and their writings. After he had first been thoroughly trained for it, he made his translation. He was moved not by the right motive, but [by the desire] so to distort certain of the words occurring in the translation of the seventy-two.

('*Treatise on Weights and Measures*' ['*De Mensuris et Ponderibus*']. *The translation is from* The Syriac Version, *edited and translated by J. E. Dean, University of Chicago Press, Chicago, 1935, pp. 30–1. This interesting text is unique in ascribing the supervision of Aelia Capitolina to Aquila, the famous translator of the Bible into Greek. It contains interesting details about Jerusalem of the first century* AD *and the status of the Jews and Christians there.*)

1 Isaiah 1 : 8
2 the famous translator of the Bible into Greek
3 a city of the Decapolis in Trans-Jordan

The medal struck by the Israeli government to commemorate the discoveries made in the Cave of Letters

Glossary

AM-HA'ARES Literally: *People of the land. Rabbinic usage for the unlearned and untrustworthy
to follow scrupulously the religious laws*

ARAMAIC *A Semitic language, akin to Hebrew*

'ARAVA *Willow. One of the 'Four Kinds', used in the Succoth*

BAR, BEN *Son. (Aramaic and Hebrew respectively)*

ELUL *Twelfth month*

ETHROG *Citron. One of the 'Four Kinds', used in the Succoth*

GEMARA *Comments and discussions of the Mishna. The Talmud consists of the Mishna and Gemara together*

HADAS *Myrtle. One of the 'Four Kinds', used in the Succoth*

HALAKHA *Religious rule*

'IYYAR *Eighth month*

KETHUBA *Marriage contract*

KIBBUTZ *A collective settlement in modern Israel where property is held in common*

KISLEV *Third month*

KOR *A measure*

LAG BA'OMER *The 33rd day in the seven week period of counting the 'omer (sheaf cut in the barley harvest),
starting from the second day of Passover to Pentecost (Leviticus 22:15)*

LETEK *A measure*

LULAV *Palm branch. One of the 'Four Kinds', used in the Succoth*

MARHESHVAN *Second month*

MENORAH *Candelabrum*

MIDRASH *Exegesis of the Bible*

MISHNA *Code of religious laws promulgated by Judah the Prince (c. AD 200). See also Gemara, Talmud, Tosefta*

MOSHAV *A settlement, with some elements of collective property, in modern Israel*

NAHAL *A dry river, canyon (Wadi in Arabic)*

NASI *President, or Prince*

NISAN *Seventh month*

RABBI *A title of a sage or teacher*

SE'AH *A measure*

SEL'A *Tetradrachma – four zuzim (dinarii)*

SHALOM *Peace, greetings*

SHEMITTAH *Remission year, Sabbatical year*

SHEVAT *Third month*

SISITH *Fringe of the* Talith

SUCCOTH *The feast of booths, or tabernacles*

TALITH *An outer shawl or mantle. Nowadays prayer shawl*

TALMUD *The Mishna and Gemara together (c. AD 200–500)*

TAMUZ *Tenth month*

TEFILLIN *Phylacteries*

TISHRI *First month*

TKHELETH *Tyrian purple*

TOSEFTA *Supplement to the Mishna*

ZUZ *Dinarius*

Bibliography   *Selected recent publications*

General

S. Yeivin,
The War of Bar-Kokhba (Hebrew),
JERUSALEM (second edition) 1952
Full treatment of all literary and archaeological
sources known prior to the latest discoveries in the
Judaean Desert

S. Abramsky,
Bar-Kokhba, President of Israel (Hebrew),
TEL-AVIV 1961
Some of the recent finds are taken into account;
see there for earlier bibliography

Joseph A. Fitzmyer, S J,
'The Bar Kochba Period',
in *Saint Mary's Theology Studies*, 1,
NEW YORK 1962, pp. 133–68
A brief but excellent treatment of the historical
sources and some of the newly found documents;
see there for previous bibliography

H. Mantel,
'The Causes of the Bar Kokhba Revolt',
The Jewish Quarterly Review, 58, 1968,
pp. 224–42; 274–96
Presenting the view that Hadrian's decrees were
the result of the revolt and not its cause; summary of
other views and further bibliography

A. Fuks,
'Aspects of the Jewish Revolt in AD 115–17',
The Journal of Roman Studies, 51, 1961, pp. 98–104
A fully-documented survey of the Diaspora Revolt
prior to the Bar-Kokhba war

Ch. Raphael
The Walls of Jerusalem
NEW YORK 1968
A good treatment of the Jewish sources

Coins and Documents

Y. Meshorer,
Jewish Coins of the Second Temple Period,
TEL-AVIV, 1967
Full treatment of all the known types
of Bar-Kokhba coins

Elisabeth Koffmahn,
Die Doppelurkunden aus der Wüste Juda,
LEIDEN, 1968

The Discoveries at Wadi Murabba'at

P. Benoit, OP, J. T. Milik, R. de Vaux, OP,
Les Grottes de Murabba'at,
(Discoveries in the Judaean Desert II),
OXFORD, 1961
The official and comprehensive report
of the finds and documents

Other Finds in the Judaean Desert (Expeditions A–C)

N. Avigad, Y. Aharoni, P. Bar-Adon,
in 'The Expedition to the Judaean Desert', 1960–1',
The Israel Exploration Journal, 11, 1961 and 12, 1962

The Cave of Letters

Y. Yadin,
in 'The Expedition to the Judaean Desert 1960–1,
The Israel Exploration Journal, 11, 1961 and 12, 1962

Y. Yadin,
The Finds from the Bar-Kokhba Period in the Cave of Letters
(Judaean Desert Studies I),
JERUSALEM, 1963
The official and comprehensive report
of the finds (excluding documents)

Masada and the Dead Sea Scrolls

Y. Yadin,
Masada – Herod's Fortress and the Zealots' Last Stand,
Weidenfeld & Nicolson,
LONDON, 1966

NOTE *Futher general treatment of the Bar-Kokhba
discoveries are to be found in most of the popular books
dealing with the Dead Sea Scrolls*

Publisher's acknowledgements

Engraving from Trajan's column on page 16:
New York Public Library, Print Division

Frescoes from the Dura Europos synagogue on
pages 72 and 78: E. R. Goodenough,
*Jewish Symbols in the Greco-Roman Period, Volume II:
Symbols in the Dura Synagogue* (Bollingen Series XXXVII,
New York, 1964) colour plate IX, detail.
Copyright © by Bollingen Foundation.
By permission of Princeton University Press.

Index compiled by Mrs Orly Ofrath

The author and publisher would like to thank
Y. Meshorer who helped in selecting the coins
for the plates.

Index